THE DISSENTING VOICE

THE TEXAS PAN AMERICAN SERIES

THE DISSENTING VOICE:

The New Essay of Spanish America, 1960–1985

MARTIN S. STABB

UNIVERSITY OF TEXAS PRESS, AUSTIN

Requests for permission to reproduce material from this work should be sent to Permissions, University of Texas Press, Box 7819, Austin, TX 78713-7819.

⊛ The paper used in this publication meets the minimum requirements of American National Standard for Information Sciences—Permanence of Paper for Printed Library Materials, ANSI Z39.48-1984.

LIBRARY OF CONGRESS CATALOGING-IN-PUBLICATION DATA

Stabb, Martin S.
　　The dissenting voice : the new essay of Spanish America, 1960–1985 /
Martin S. Stabb. — 1st ed.
　　　　p.　　cm. — (The Texas Pan American series)
　　Includes bibliographical references and index.
　　ISBN 0-292-77684-5 (alk. paper)
　　1. Spanish American essays—History and criticism.　2. Spanish American prose
literature—20th century—History and criticism.　I. Title.　II. Series.
PQ7082.E8S83　1994
864—dc20　　　　　　　　　　　　　　　　　　　　　　　93-44720

Permission to quote extensively from Octavio Paz, *The Monkey Grammarian*, trans. Helen Lane (copyright © 1974 by Editorial Seix Barral, S. A.; translation copyright © 1981 by Seaver Books, New York, N.Y.), courtesy of Seaver Books and Peter Owen Publishers, London.

Contents

Acknowledgments

A great deal of the material, thematic interrelationships, and organizational ideas that form this study came out of discussions in my graduate seminar on the Spanish American essay; hence, I owe a basic debt to my students.

I am also indebted to a number of individuals who have contributed to this project: to my colleague Terry Peavler, with whom I have had many fruitful discussions especially regarding Julio Cortázar, to Roselyn Costantino, also of Penn State, for valuable suggestions regarding the essays of Rosario Castellanos; to Karen Connelly and Donna Campbell, who successfully transformed my first draft to the word processor; to my wife, Gloria, who read proof and helped rectify stylistic quirks and questionable sentence structure.

I am especially indebted to the Penn State Institute for the Arts and Humanistic Studies for their financial support at a crucial stage in the project's development.

I also wish to thank the publishers of *Hispania* for permission to incorporate into the present study considerable material from my article "The New Essay of Mexico: Text and Context." Likewise, I must thank the publishers of the *Hispanic Review* for permission to use a substantial portion of my article "Not Text but Texture: Cortázar and the New Essay." Finally, I wish to thank Seaver Books (Arcade Publishing) and Peter Owen Publishers, London, for permission to quote extensively from their excellent translation, *The Monkey Grammarian*, by Octavio Paz.

A Note on Translations

Unless otherwise noted, all the translations into English are my own. Following my first citation of original Spanish titles I include, within parentheses, the English translation of the work. In the case of works which have been published in translation, the English version is in italics with conventional capitalization: otherwise, I simply indicate a rough translation, which appears in normal type. My bibliography makes no attempt to include all the available translations of Spanish American essays. I do, however, list those quoted in the text and a few others of particular interest.

Introduction

ONE

Some time ago when I first addressed the question of the development of the Spanish American essay, I focused on a seventy-year period (1890–1960) and I placed my emphasis on what I called the essay of ideas, almost to the exclusion of more formal, aesthetic aspects of the genre. In fact, some historian friends, as well as many colleagues in literature, suggested that what I really had produced was a book in the area of intellectual or cultural history.

The present study differs substantially, though not entirely, from my earlier work. In the first place I have limited myself to a shorter and to what at least appeared to be a more manageable period, 1960 to 1985. Second, I have dealt with a greater variety of texts, including a number of works that would hardly be considered essays in terms of a strict definition of the genre. This no-man's-land of "essayistic" writing—collage, testimonials, diaries, poetic prose, and other hybrid forms—cannot be ignored simply because it does not fit easily into well-established formal categories. I trust that by including some texts of this type I am not guilty of using the term "essay" as a "catch-all for [all] non-fiction prose works of limited length," to cite Robert Scholes and Carl Klaus.[1] Rather, I hope that the examination of these seemingly peripheral writings may well sharpen our understanding of the nature and limits of this notoriously ill-defined genre.

The word "dissent" in my title characterizes, I believe, the work of almost all the essayists discussed, though it clearly is more appropriate in some cases than in others. It certainly describes the position of those writers (like recent Nobel laureate Octavio Paz) who, despite earlier allegiance to—or flirtation with—the left, dissent sharply from what for many years had been ideological orthodoxy among Latin American intellectuals. It also fits the case of others who continued to maintain a leftist orientation yet whose departure from the political canon and whose critique of Marxist regimes have set them apart from official parties and programs. But dissent has not been limited to attacks against the left. The Mexican essayists, for example, have frequently censured their nation's nominally democratic government for its reliance on single-party politics, its bureaucracy, and its thinly veiled conservatism. The term also describes a number of writers who have taken a dissenting position in the face of the pervasive, fashionable cult of "development," of bigness for bigness' sake. Finally, several of the essayists under examination—those whose work will be treated in my final chapter dealing with what I have called "the new essay"— can be thought of as dissenters in a purely literary sense. That is, they take issue with the traditional view that the essay should be an unambiguous, lineally ordered piece of expository prose, presented by a single authorial voice. In some cases this kind of aesthetic dissidence and ideological dissent are conjoined in the work of the same author, producing what one such writer, Julio Cortázar, called "Che Guevaras of language."

As before, the realities of literary activity suggest certain geographic centers—notably Mexico City and Buenos Aires—as being more important than others, and so writers from these places figure more prominently than the Cubans, Peruvians, Venezuelans, and others. I must make clear, however, that I have not sought to focus the present study on representative essayists of one nation or another. It should be remembered that during the period under examination a number of Spanish Americans were writing in exile, that professional and personal contacts between writers of different nationalities became increasingly frequent, and that publishing (witness the role of Barcelona in this regard) was becoming steadily more international. The result has been shared experience, cross-fertilization in essayistic form as well as in content, and the production of texts that are as interesting for their broad hemispheric concerns as they are for what they reveal of specific, national issues.

It should be helpful at this point to review some of these hemispheric concerns of the decades under study. In general the 1960s began on a decidedly optimistic note. From the Hispanic American viewpoint heroes—both political and cultural—were not hard to find: Fidel Castro's revolutionary regime was only a year old and enjoyed widespread support, especially among the intellectuals. Although a few traditionally vicious dictatorships persisted in such places as Paraguay, Nicaragua, or the Dominican Republic, the larger countries were, with varying degrees of success, pursuing the paths of democracy. A number of "strong men" of previous decades—Pérez Jiménez, Perón, Rojas Pinilla, Odría—were being replaced by more enlightened leaders—Betancourt,

Frondizi, Belaúnde Terry, and others. While endemic social and economic problems persisted beneath the surface in many areas, the hemisphere's material progress, especially in the rapidly growing urban zones, was impressive. A country like Mexico—with its new skyscrapers and magnificent University City complex—is perhaps the clearest example of the growing emphasis upon "development" in all its physical and social connotations. Other cities such as Caracas or Lima were not far behind.

The spirit of change and innovation suggested by democratization and development was underscored in the cultural sphere, especially among the writers. The late 1950s and especially the 1960s saw Spanish American literature emerge from its status as picturesque, peripheral, "Third World" writing—of considerable documentary value but only of minor aesthetic interest—to take its place at the very frontiers of international literary activity. Argentina's Jorge Luis Borges, a unique and solitary figure, appears to have been the first to achieve this level of recognition, but he was soon followed by a brilliant group of narrators: Carlos Fuentes, Mario Vargas Llosa, Gabriel García Márquez, Julio Cortázar, and a number of others. These men, several of whom produced important essayistic texts as well as novels and short stories, all tended toward the left and at least in the early 1960s were enthusiastic supporters of Castro and the new Cuba. Indeed Havana, with its active literary life, its highly publicized book prizes, and its government-supported publishing enterprises, briefly became the hemispheric interface between cultural innovation and political commitment.

But the early and mid-1960s was an ambiguous period and one which still remains difficult to characterize, especially with regard to the younger generation. On the one hand, Spanish America's youth seems to have been deeply moved by the image of Cuba, the Latin David standing up to the Yankee Goliath; on the other, the insidious appeal of North American popular culture, especially in its rock and roll, blue jeans, and youth liberation manifestations, molded—some would say corrupted—the soul of Latin America's youth. There may have been some significance in the fact that during the 1960s almost every kiosk in the area seemed to be doing its best trade in two items: a bigger-than-life poster of the young Che Guevara and a similar one of the youthful John F. Kennedy. I stress this almost schizophrenic attitude toward the United States evident in the hemisphere's younger generation because the theme of the youth (or student) movement along with the question of North America as a model becomes central in the work of several essayists of the period.

As the decade moved on, however, a good deal of the earlier years' optimism began to wane. For one thing, democratic regimes in several countries, Argentina and Peru, for example, were tottering: by the second half of the 1960s both nations would see the return of military governments. Little Uruguay, for years considered a model of political and social progress, witnessed a marked shift to the right, fueled by fears that its economy could no longer afford the luxury of a welfare state. Mexico, while retaining its image of democracy and "revolutionary institutions," was beset by political cynicism and a soon-to-surface restlessness among its youth that would manifest itself in the dramatic and bloody confrontation of 1968.

Events in Cuba show, in a slightly different way, a negative turn during the middle and late 1960s. The euphoria and unconditional support that the regime inspired worldwide among many intellectuals began to erode in the face of Castro's increasing pressures for conformity on the part of writers and artists. When the blatant Padilla affair began to develop in 1967 several of Spanish America's most celebrated authors (the "new novelists" Fuentes and Vargas Llosa, for example) became openly critical of the Cuban regime. In short, the honeymoon between Castro and Spanish America's literati was, for many of the latter, over. Essayists especially were sensitive to this turn of events and bear witness to what might be considered the loss of political innocence among intellectuals.

With only a limited number of exceptions, the close of the decade was characterized by uncertainties and increasing gloom. Events in Mexico, especially the Tlatelolco massacre alluded to above, cast doubts over that nation's political and cultural life which have persisted till the present. Democracy sputtered in Peru with the overthrow of President Belaúnde Terry and the installation of what many—including some intellectuals—hoped would be a radically different revolutionary regime. However, only a few years after its establishment it too became just another military government unable to fulfill the promises of its nationalist-Marxist rhetoric. Authoritarianism and dictatorship became increasingly entrenched in Argentina and Uruguay, while Stroessner and the Somoza clan maintained their grip on Paraguay and Nicaragua, respectively. The largest country in the hemisphere, Brazil (which, it should be noted, is not included in this study), was also being ruled by an increasingly harsh military.

The trend toward political repression gathered strength during the 1970s, especially in the Southern Cone. The Allende government of Chile—unique in that it was a democratically elected Marxist regime—remained in power less than three years: its violent overthrow in 1973 had considerable U.S. support and led to the iron-fisted dictatorship of General Pinochet. In Argentina, after a brief and absurd return of Peronism, the military tightened its bloody grip on the nation, abetted by a vicious system of quasi-official counter-guerrilla groups. Uruguay, Peru, and Brazil fared no better. In the 1970s the simple

Spanish word *desaparecido* (disappeared) acquired a new, decidedly ominous meaning. The decade also witnessed the flight of many Spanish American intellectuals, as well as ordinary citizens, to safer havens in Europe, the United States, or those Latin American nations where writers could work in a relatively unthreatening environment. Indeed, one can speak of an exile subculture during the period within which several important essayists may be counted: their work bears eloquent testimony to the plight of the alienated and dispossessed.

Problems of a political nature were not the only ones that plagued the continent during the 1970s. The rapid growth of the economy in many areas, though greeted enthusiastically at first, soon gave rise to a number of serious concerns. Essayists especially were quick to note the inequities of development and its disruptive effect on certain sectors of the population. Perhaps most of all, writers were sensitive to the mindless cult of technology and progress that it fostered. Nowhere are these reactions to *desarrollismo* better seen than in Mexico, where fluctuating oil prices, runaway urban growth, and wild investments produced a generation of nouveaux riches waiting to be dissected and lampooned by ever-vigilant writers. While these phenomena were not quite as evident in some countries, economics certainly underlay a number of major concerns of Spanish America's essayists: in addition to the themes noted above, questions of economic dependency, the endemic problem of rural poverty, environmental threats, and so on all surface in their texts.

The waning years of the period under consideration are so recent that any interpretations of trends and tendencies must be viewed as rather tentative. As for politics, the late 1970s and the first half of the 1980s bode well for supporters of democracy: Argentina, Peru, Ecuador, and Brazil all saw the demise of military government. The Chilean dictatorship began moving toward a return to representative government and the Somoza regime of Nicaragua was toppled by a revolutionary junta—one that came under attack by the United States for its Marxist leanings but which, as recent events have shown, permitted a broad spectrum of political participation. Democracy, at least the single, dominant party version of the system, continued to function in Mexico, albeit under increasing criticism from intellectuals and rival political groups. Representative government, despite difficult local problems, has been maintained in a number of other countries—Venezuela, Colombia, and elsewhere. Little has happened in Cuba, though Castro's charismatic aura seems to have been growing dimmer. Whether Cuba will follow the course of the socialist countries of Eastern Europe, whose former regimes it resembles in some respects, remains to be seen. The ideological issues raised by these recent shifts in Spanish American politics—basic questions relating to democracy, authoritarianism, Marxism, and capitalism—have, not surprisingly, been subjects of lively debate by essayists throughout the two and a half decades under examination. However, it appears that by the mid-1980s the kind of abstract ideological polemics of earlier years was waning. Debate and discussion persist, but many writers seem to take positions on more pragmatic, issue-oriented grounds.

In the foregoing review of recent affairs in Spanish America I noted how essayists often reflected the problems and concerns of the period. At this point, however, a brief examination of 1960 to 1985 in terms of the literary setting is in order. As we have already noted, the 1960s witnessed the coming of age of the hemisphere's literature. Foreshadowed by the remarkable figure of Jorge Luis Borges, the celebrated "new novelists" dazzled the world with their brilliant innovative fiction. Clearly it was the work of writers like García Márquez, Fuentes, Cortázar, and Vargas Llosa that gave Spanish America an unprecedented moment of literary glory. Poetry, too, contributed to the continent's literary achievement, but even in the case of Nobel laureate Pablo Neruda, it seemed to represent the culmination of trends begun decades earlier, rather than new directions.

Although the originality and creative intensity of the new narrative appeared to be fading by the 1970s, the impact of the movement upon essayistic prose should not be underestimated. For one thing, a number of the new novelists also wrote essays or texts closely akin to this genre. For another, the technical innovations of one genre tend to be contagious, affecting other related literary forms, especially when the dominant genre has enjoyed great success. This process has, in my view, produced a body of writing that can with some justification be considered *nuevo ensayismo* paralleling the more celebrated *nueva narrativa*. I do not wish to give the impression that all recent essayistic writing of the hemisphere falls into this category: fairly traditional essays continue to appear and even the same writer may choose at times to write a relatively old-fashioned essay and at others to experiment with more innovative forms. One such figure is Octavio Paz, whose dual talents as poet and cultural critic are brilliantly reflected in his essays. Perhaps more than any other single author his voice—unequivocally one of dissent—dominates the pages of this study.

Although I have centered my attention on the idea of dissent as applied to a limited number of themes and have left the discussion of contemporary essayistic techniques to be considered in only a single chapter, I nonetheless believe that this study provides a useful point of departure for further investigation of writers and themes, some of which are only briefly treated here. Though it is not a general survey of the contemporary Spanish American essay, it should be of considerable value to students of the hemisphere's literature and to Latin Americanists in related fields. No doubt some significant writers and some important texts have been omitted.[2] For example, additional women essayists might well have been included in this study. Although I deal with Rosario Castellanos at some length and mention Victoria Ocampo in passing, writers such as Mexico's Margo Glantz, Puerto Rico's Rosario Ferré, and others have produced texts that fall within the bounds of essayistic writing broadly defined. The contribution of women writers to the essay is, however, being investigated elsewhere, and I look forward to seeing the results of this activity. Conceivably another researcher using a different approach and other criteria for selection might produce a valid but yet rather dissimilar work covering the same general area. I suspect that these possibilities are inherent in any project that attempts to find some order in the seeming chaos of very recent letters, especially in the case of the essay—that illusive, often hybrid creature that one of its finest cultivators, Alfonso Reyes, termed "ese centauro de los géneros" (that centaur of genres).

Revolution or Rebellion?

T W O

Octavio Paz (1914–   ), unquestionably one of contemporary Spanish America's most perceptive essayists, has frequently pointed out the important yet easily overlooked difference between the terms "revolution" and "rebellion." In such major collections as *Corriente alterna* (*Alternating Current*, 1967), *Los hijos del limo* (*Children of the Mire*, 1972), and *Tiempo nublado* (Cloudy times, 1983), he notes that a revolution seeks the replacement of one regime by another, whereas a rebellion aims at overthrowing existing authority but tends to be unclear or open-ended regarding what might replace the defeated system. Not surprisingly, he finds that recent years are characterized more by rebellion than revolution: "This indifference toward the shape the future should take distinguishes the new radicalism from the revolutionary movements of the nineteenth century and first half of the twentieth." The Mexican essayist then goes on to note that "confidence in the strength of spontaneity exists in inverse proportion to the disgust toward systematic constructs."[1] Others parallel the ideas to a considerable degree. Thus Argentine essayist and novelist Ernesto Sábato (1911–   ), speaking of writers, observes that "they are at heart antisocial, rebels, and therefore they frequently are sympathetic toward revolutionary movements. But when revolutions triumph, it is not unusual for them to become rebels again."[2] In other words, the rebellious spirit tends to be a constant force, often "indifferent" to the future or distrustful of the systems that revolutions strive to establish. Although Spanish America has had some very real revolutions and although the political climate of much of the area has often been considered revolutionary, the term "rebellion" appears to describe more accurately the literary situation of the region's writers and perhaps that of the culture as a whole. At least the evidence provided by the essay points in this direction.

While much of this rebellious ferment has clearly been political in nature, the essayists suggest that the phenomenon has been much broader. Paz, for example, writes in *Los hijos del limo* that at heart it represents a reaction against Western capitalist values and specifically the "moral code of savings and work." He refines this idea by describing the trend as "the insurrection of corporal and orgiastic values . . . a rebellion against man's twofold penalty—condemnation to work and repression of desire" (*CM*, 155–156). He further notes that in the worldwide student movements of the 1960s youth was rebelling against the "excessive rationality of life" (*CM*, 153). To what extent do these perceptions provide insight into phenomena that others may have treated only superficially, or to what extent do they merely represent idiosyncratic views of reality shaped by certain long-standing attitudes frequently noted in Paz's work?[3] Stated more concretely, were the students who protested at Berkeley, at the Sorbonne, at the National University or Polytechnic in Mexico, and elsewhere inspired by well-defined political models (such as that provided by Castro and the Cubans), or were they rebelling against the "excessive rationality of life" and the "repressing of desire"?

A number of other essayists offer answers to these and related questions. Julio Cortázar (1914–1984), though usually remembered as a masterful writer of fiction but who also must be reckoned with as a prolific and innovative essayist, has commented upon the youth movement in several texts. His unique essayistic collage, "Noticias del mes de mayo" (News of the month of May), published in *Ultimo round* (The final round, 1969), attempts to evoke the spirit of Parisian youth—and by extension all the young rebels of the period—during the heady days of protest in the spring of 1968. His opening lines of poetic prose describe the students' struggle as that of "a handful of kids against the Tried and True."[4] His citation of slogans and graffiti, an essential part of his text, stresses the emotive, often sexually charged nature of the movement rather than any specifically political material. Thus he includes such proclamations as "my desires are reality"; "unbutton your mind as frequently as your fly"; "the rules imposed against pleasure excite the pleasure of living without rules"; "the more I make love the more I want to make revolution"; or the delightfully brief "prohibiting is prohibited" (*UR*, 47–59). In this kind of essay the author makes no neat summations or conclusions, yet his message is clear: although the youthful activists of 1968 had some specific short-term goals and although their political orientation was generally toward the left, the force that powered the movement was a profound desire to shake up the establishment, to undermine the older generation's faith in the "Tried and True" (my translation of

Cortázar's phrase *la Gran Costumbre*), to liberate themselves from the taboos and restrictions of an overly mechanized, overly rational society. There is every indication, moreover, that Cortázar sympathizes wholeheartedly with these attitudes.

Though Argentine by virtue of his parentage and early life, it is somewhat difficult to consider Cortázar (who spent most of his adult years in France) an ideal observer of his country. However, essayists closer to home have certainly reflected the same interest in the phenomenon of revolt, especially as it was manifest among Spanish America's restless and rapidly growing youth. Several fellow Argentines, such as Julio Mafud (1928–   ) and Juan José Sebreli (1930–   ), take passing note of these matters, though unlike Cortázar they are critical rather than sympathetic toward the new generation. These two essayists, writing in the late 1960s, find that on balance younger people are insincere, terribly spoiled by indulgent parents, and the willing victims of materialistic manipulation.[5] Their restiveness, what there is of it, seems to be perceived more as a whimper than as a cry of genuine rebellion. The fact that Argentine essayists do not appear to have become very deeply involved literarily or emotionally with the youth movement is of some significance: it suggests that in socially conservative Argentina the younger generation's protest was muted, that the rebelliousness typical of the mid- and late 1960s was minimal.[6] By comparison with other countries (Mexico, for example), the Argentine treatment of this theme—except for the work of the exile Cortázar—is not especially impressive.

Perhaps the perspective gained by expatriates yields richer insights than those obtained by writers who remain at home. The career of Uruguay's Eduardo Galeano (1940–   ) may support this view. Like a number of other writers of the period under examination, Galeano has spent much of his life living and working as an exile from his homeland. In many respects his poetic— at times erotic—prose, his strident denunciation of exploitation in Latin America, and his life as a wondering radical make him an archetypical representative of the rebels of the 1960s and 1970s. The very titles of his most celebrated collections underscore this role: *Las venas abiertas de la América Latina* (*The Open Veins of Latin America*, 1971) and *Días y noches de amor y guerra* (Days and nights of love and war, 1978). On a number of occasions he has touched upon the themes of youth and rebellion. A committed leftist, he typically points out how even the apparent dissent of the hemisphere's youth movement has been corrupted by the values of the highly developed capitalist world. A good example of these concerns is seen in his comments during a discussion with students in Quito, Ecuador: "The symbols and fetishes of the North American youth revolt of the sixties are now being mass produced in the developed world.

Clothing with psychedelic designs is being sold to the cry of 'Freedom!' and big business is flooding the Third World with music, posters, hair styles and garments that reproduce aesthetic images of hallucination by drugs." He goes on to point out that the Spanish American young people who consume these goods are merely posturing, that all this simply represents "adventures for those who are paralyzed: reality is left untouched, only its image is changed."[7] It should be borne in mind, nonetheless, that Galeano's critique of the young rebels is that of a very sympathetic observer. His work leaves little doubt that he supports and identifies with the youth movement. The fact that it has been manipulated and defused by the ever-present enemy is what concerns him.

A somewhat different perspective of Latin America's new radicalism is presented by Carlos Rangel (1930–1988), a Venezuelan journalist, television personality, and author of a highly charged political essay, *Del buen salvaje al buen revolucionario* (*The Latin Americans: Their Love-Hate Relationship with the United States*, 1976). This book, which was publicly burned by outraged university students, is much more than an analysis of the hemisphere's revolutionary movements. Writing in a no-holds-barred journalistic style, Rangel makes a frontal assault upon virtually all of Latin America's most cherished notions regarding the continent's lack of progress, its dependency, its role as victim of Yankee imperialism, and so on. Many of the positions he attacks are, of course, basic tenets of the left. Space does not permit a detailed analysis of the essay's many strengths and perhaps more numerous weaknesses. In general terms, however, Rangel makes a fairly strong case for his thesis that Latin Americans have been too eager to place the blame for their social, economic, and political problems upon external forces, the most obvious of which is the United States.

The subtitles of the book's first chapter are almost sufficient in themselves to give the general lines of the author's argument: "From the Indies to the Paradise of This World"; "The New World, Utopia"; "The Noble Savage"; "Civilization"; "The Noble Revolutionary"; "The Reverse of Myths." As these headings indicate, Rangel treads familiar ground. Beginning with the discovery, he points out how the myth of the Noble Savage and its corollary utopian myth developed and spread. Early in the chapter he makes a basic point, one that seems to be quite consistent with the utopian thought of writers such as Martínez Estrada, Paz, and Cortázar: "to understand the transformation of the Noble Savage into the Noble Revolutionary, we must note that there is not merely a relationship, but rather identity between the state of man before the fall and after salvation . . . The final days will be like the first ones; the end of history will be the return of the Golden Age."[8] Rangel interprets this kind of utopianism in very negative terms, and his sharp criticism of the Spanish American left derives directly from this position. In his view, the underlying motif of a "return" smacks of religious fanaticism not unlike the *milenarismo* of certain primitive religious sects. Moreover, it accounts for the unrealistic, essentially atavistic appeal of the continent's charismatic prophets and martyrs of the extreme left—figures such as Che Guevara, Camilo Torres, and the like. At its core, Rangel observes, this kind of looking backward is simply a conven-ient consolation for those who feel themselves to be "pushed into the past, marginalized, frustrated, defeated, dispossessed of their *natural* right to the same enjoyment of the fruits of the land that the Noble Savages of America supposedly enjoyed before the arrival of the fateful caravels" (*BR*, 30).

Rangel is particularly vitriolic in his criticism of universities, where, he claims, self-interested faculty members exist in a "symbiotic parasitic" rela-tionship with superficial, intellectually lazy students and where professing "revolutionary" ideology is de rigueur. He delights in pointing out that uni-versity students typically perpetuate their middle- or upper-class status, that their revolutionary rhetoric seldom results in any concrete benefits for the lower classes, and that their radical activities constitute a kind of game in which the players are at little or no personal risk: "to be 'revolutionary' in a Latin American university is more or less as heterodox and as risky as being a fervent Catholic in an Irish seminary" (*BR*, 192).

Our consideration of revolution and rebellion began with some general observations by Mexico's foremost essayist. However, Octavio Paz is only one of an impressive group of his compatriots to examine these themes: in fact, Mexico provides some of the richest material on the new rebels, the youth movement, social revolution, and related questions to be found in the hemi-sphere. An important group of younger writers, some of whom would take sharp issue with Paz's views on revolution and other matters, emerged in the sixties as the interpreters of the nation's social and political restiveness. The group includes, among others, Carlos Monsiváis (1938–   ), whose age and interest at the time make him very close to the youth movement he so vividly describes in such works as *Días de guardar* (Days to cherish, 1970) and *Amor perdido* (Lost love, 1978); Juan García Ponce (1932–   ), some of whose best essays are collected in *Desconsideraciones* (Inconsiderations, 1968); and Alberto Dallal (1936–   ), critic of the arts, whose *Gozosa revolución* (Joyous revolution, 1973) bears directly on our central themes. Of slightly different orientation though generationally related to the group are such writers as Gabriel Zaid (1934–   ), whose major collections include *Como leer en bicicleta* (How to read on a bicycle, 1975, 1979) and *El progreso improductivo* (Nonproductive progress, 1979); celebrated novelist Carlos Fuentes (1929–   ), author of a number of essays among which the collection *Tiempo mexicano* (Mexican time, 1971) is perhaps the most significant;[9] and the late Jorge Ibargüengoitia (1928–1983), whose sly comments in *Viajes en la América ignota* (Travels in unknown America, 1972) constitute delightful informal essays.

The relationship of these writers to the essayists who preceded them—especially to the Paz of the 1940s and 1950s—is clarified to some degree by philosopher and scholar Luis Villoro, who wrote of the intellectuals emerging in the 1960's, "a characteristic symptom of the moment is the lack of interest, especially among the younger generation, in those themes that were of such great concern to my generation."[10] The themes referred to as not interesting to the new writers were those of "self-knowledge" and the "Philosophy of Mexicanness"—key issues in the writings of Paz and the Hiperión group of the preceding decade. What then were the specific preoccupations of these writers? Fuentes, in his comment of 1963, sheds some light on this question. The writers of the decade, he notes, may be characterized by "not delving into the abstract idea of 'Mexicanness' but rather into the concrete nature of Mexicans, socially or individually considered."[11] What Fuentes appears to be saying here is of considerable help in understanding the emerging essayists of the period. Unlike earlier generations who, at least in retrospect, seem to have been dominated by a controlling idea (as in the case of the turn-of-the-century positivists), these essayists were not ideologues. Rather, they responded to concrete situations and current trends in the world of accelerated change that characterizes the second half of this century. Thus, Juan García Ponce writing on the apparently unrelated subject of Mexican cinema notes that the interest in tracing national idiosyncrasies is no longer very fascinating, that "this serious task was the subject of earlier generations' concern, but now we must be up to date."[12] At times, the new essayists appear to be almost flippant in defining their generational outlook: thus Monsiváis, writing in 1967 on the new generation in Mexico, will enumerate their concerns as "fashions in clothes, songs, protest authors, neckties, dance styles."[13] Of course, the early and mid-sixties was a unique period in Mexico as elsewhere. The youth movement, from Berkeley to Paris to the Pedregal, was in its heyday, high fashion (the miniskirt, "swinging London," etc.) had become a worldwide cult. Pop culture—especially rock music—was making unprecedented inroads on the general society and, on a somewhat more serious level, the Spanish American "boom" in fiction was under way. Fuentes, like Monsiváis, is a good barometer of the times: in "Carlos Fuentes habla de su vida" (Carlos Fuentes speaks about his life), a profusely illustrated confessional essay of 1965, he paints a picture of high-flying literary life. He notes that a single article sold to foreign (especially U.S.) publications produces more revenue than an entire novel published in Mexico; that he is a "chronic cinema-addict"; that he has many female admirers; that he enjoys his comfortable home in fashionable San Angel; and finally, that while he considers Marxism "a rich but partial interpretation of existence," he does not believe that it is "an obligation of writers to swell the ranks of the needy."[14]

This rather freewheeling frivolous mood of the mid-1960s was perhaps superficial and was certainly short-lived. As in Europe and North America, the new freedom claimed by the younger generation was to lead to an inevitable confrontation with the establishment: in the case of Mexico, this took the form of the Tlatelolco student massacre and its aftermath. These events and their background became central themes of the new essayists and major determinants of their generational identity. The mood of the times is best appreciated in the light of Mexican political history since the mid-century, a period which witnessed the continuing—if not accelerating—growth of power by the PRI, a political force whose pervasive style has become unique in Latin America.[15] The presence of a highly bureaucratized, manipulative regime whose "revolutionary" rhetoric often seemed hollow in the light of its specific policies and its parade of mediocre chief executives was becoming increasingly irksome to the intellectuals, especially since many of them earned their livelihood either directly or indirectly through government-funded positions.

No one more than Carlos Monsiváis reflects the mood of the times. A prolific writer, his books and numerous essays in periodicals deal with popular culture (cinema, comics, Mexican foibles, celebrities, popular music), high culture (especially poetry), politics, the youth movement, generational conflict, sexual revolution, technology, urbanism, and a host of related subjects. Given this extremely broad range of themes, it is difficult to generalize about his fundamental positions and attitudes; all the more so since his authorial tone runs the full gamut from a kind of literary stand-up comedian to that of the intense, angry young man. However, even in his comic mode this self-professed "mixture of Albert Camus and Ringo Starr"[16] has much of substance to say. Perhaps the unifying themes found in his work have been the affirmation of change and of what might be termed a defense of cultural populism versus the establishment. Clearly these are the underlying motifs in his successful book-length collection *Días de guardar*: note, for example, the chapter "My Friends and I" in which he lashes out against *el México visible*: "the sum total of titles . . . distinctions, prizes . . . academics . . . model households . . . Rotarians, Lions . . . union leaders, ex-ministers."[17] His joyful recounting of the triumphs of La Onda (literally, the wave) during the sixties youth movement is another facet of the same theme. In this regard, representative texts would be his piece on neologisms and youth slang, "Sobre el significado de la palabra 'huato' " (On the meaning of the word *huato*), his comments on one of several Mexican rock concerts of the period, "Para todas las cosas hay sazón" (For all things there is a season), or his earlier overview "México, 1967," a rich analysis of the mood of the times wherein Monsiváis—still in his twenties—boldly proclaims, "'The *onda* is the new spirit, the rejection of conventions and prejudices, the creation of the new morality . . . the advance of social militants . . . their yearning for another Renaissance."[18]

A number of other writers parallel Monsiváis's interest in the new culture of youth. Alberto Dallal, for example, discusses the essence of the youth movement and states that the key concept of the *here and now* represents "healthy opportunism" since it heightens reality by amplifying the vision or sense of the present.[19] In the same essay he dwells at length on the new "tenderness" (*ternura*) characteristic of interpersonal relations among the younger generation and of how this leads to better communication, better sex, and a better world.[20] In contrast to Monsiváis, Dallal presents these views quite uncritically and in a tone reminiscent of an older academic rather than that of a close contemporary of the generation he is describing. This effect is heightened by his frequent references and citations from a host of authorities ranging from Herbert Marcuse, Lewis S. Ferrer, and Antonin Artaud to Jerry Rubin and Jimi Hendrix. Some of these and other closely related issues are also raised—though in a more subtle manner—by Juan García Ponce in his collection *Desconsideraciones*. In classically titled essays such as "The Old and the New," "The Value of the Future," or "The Fashion of Fashion" García analyzes the new concepts of modernity spawned by the youth movement. Even in a totally different context, that of an essentially political essay written by a member of the older generation, Cosío Villegas's *El estilo personal de gobernar* (The personal style of governing, 1974) notes the impact of youth culture. In this case the distinguished historian presents a deliciously funny picture of President Echeverría's politically inspired attempts to appear younger and to surround himself with a youthful staff. Elsewhere in Cosío's short but very pithy journalistic essays he sets forth some nicely reasoned explanations for both the universal and specifically Mexican manifestations of the youth movement.[21]

Questions of politics, demography, La Onda, and the nature of youth culture all seem to converge in the dramatic events of 1968. Not only are the specific details of Tlatelolco described by many of the essayists, but the reaction to the tragedy has become a defining theme of the entire generation under discussion. What actually happened during the summer of 1968 and on October 3 of that year is more a matter for historians than for students of literature.[22] Very briefly, after months of mounting tension between demonstrating secondary and university students and governmental authorities, a violent confrontation occurred at the Plaza of Three Cultures in the Tlatelolco section of Mexico City. A substantial number of young people—the exact figure has become a matter of heated discussion—were killed by federal troops. While several immediate issues were involved in the confrontation, essayists like Monsiváis, Fuentes, Dallal, Paz, and others have attempted to analyze the entire affair with a view toward understanding its causes and assessing its long-term effects.

As might be expected, the general attitude expressed by these writers regarding Tlatelolco is one of sympathy with the students and outrage toward the authorities.[23] Fuentes, certainly one of the most articulate voices of the group, was deeply affected by the events of 1968. Indeed, when his occasionally flippant tone of the mid-1960s is compared with his post-Tlatelolco texts gathered together in *Tiempo mexicano*, the shift toward seriousness and sobriety is evident.

It is significant that Fuentes was in France during the spring of 1968 and that he had already witnessed and described the student movement in Paris.[24] Thus, when he discusses Tlatelolco, he places the events in a worldwide context. Recalling the Mexican confrontation suggests a kind of kinship with others involved in the struggle for justice and human dignity: "the Cuban peasants explaining their problems directly to Fidel Castro with a new sense of dignity; Parisian students fighting behind the barricades of Boulevard St. Michel to be something more than smiling robots of the consumer society; Czech workers on strike against the censorship of the press in a Prague metallurgical plant. And men like them that have resisted . . . the imposing imperial power of the United States in Vietnam."[25]

But Fuentes, as superb an essayist as he is a narrator, is quick to change his perspective, and so he rapidly moves from the wide angle of universal considerations to specific close-ups of Mexico: "A doctor friend of mine calculated that there were five hundred bodies in the morgue where he went to find his son. On locating his bullet-ridden corpse, he asked permission to remove it for burial. 'Not one cadaver leaves here,' the official answered" (*TM*, 153). Fuentes chills his readers with many other scenes equally graphic: the piles of dead students at the entrance of a church whose doors were never opened to afford refuge from the massacre, or the cynical indifference of the president, who subsequently retired to his smog-proof air-conditioned mansion where perhaps his filtered air system even kept out the "stench of blood."

But it is when he distances himself from these scenes and considers the full significance of 1968 on Mexican politics and life that his stature as a major essayist can be fully appreciated. "The events of 1968 signify for Mexico a crisis of growth, of transformation, and of conscience," he tells us. Like other crucial periods this one represents a concentration of historical currents: "everything that our country *is* came together, tacitly or overtly, in order that the movement of 1968 might be what it was" (*TM*, 145). Perhaps his most astute observations deal with the political sphere and its underlying social environment. For Fuentes, the government's violent overreaction to the students was indicative that an era was passing: the "system" of rewards, punishments, alliances, deals, and facades that the PRI had managed to erect over the years could no longer handle the pressures of the times. This inability to control the situation signified that "the system ruined itself . . . it showed that it lacked political answers to a political problem" (*TM*, 156). In a word, he warns Mexicans—especially the bourgeoisie—that they could become victims of "typical" Latin American repressive militarism—the *gorilato*—if they chose to protect the status quo and their material well-being through force rather than responsible political means.

Monsiváis, perhaps the central figure of the group, has discussed the Tlatelolco affair at great length and on many occasions. Like his colleagues, he has unequivocally stated that 1968 is an "axial year" and that much of Mexican life during the years preceding this moment of truth was, in great measure, inauthentic: "such was the situation before July of '68: worthless years, where self-deception made us act and obliged us to believe. Years of minimum intensity, made up of receptions, cocktail parties, laudatory notes" (*DG*, 74). Similar statements are not difficult to find elsewhere in Monsiváis's writing. Note, for example, his comments on Mexican society and literature in an extensive essay published in 1973: "from the formal point of view, the slaughter at the Plaza of Three Cultures reveals that the Mexican Revolution has died, and this is a political fact as well as a cultural fact . . . and therefore genuine literature should fulfill an obligation; that of clarifying the extent of our rejection and the dimensions of our . . . political, social, cultural and moral dissent."[26]

Monsiváis's interest in the student movement began early and continued well beyond the events of 1968. In a searching essay of 1966, "The Only Culture Capable of Overcoming Our Underdevelopment Has Lost a Battle," he takes a hard look at the events surrounding the student-initiated resignation of university rector Ignacio Chávez. His conclusions regarding this confrontation are especially interesting, since he finds fault on both sides. It is also significant that he distances himself from the specific situation and observes that the real tragedy lies in the fact that all parties betrayed the true nature of the university in their acceptance of "the idea . . . that has come to identify the university with a factory: that the authorities are the bosses and the students the exploited workers."[27] A similar example of his ability to see beyond the circumstantial and to place events in fresh context is seen in *Días de guardar* when he interprets the student movement as further evidence of changing life-styles and values. Here he draws upon Marshall MacLuhan and reads the movement as a text: "the message of the movement was . . . its fundamental methods: the brigades and their instinct of solidarity . . . The message of the movement was its great expressive atmosphere: the unyielding urgency of public commitment, the sense of community, the exigency of dialogue" (*DG*, 271).

The question of authorial distancing becomes crucial in the case of Octavio Paz's rendering of Tlatelolco and the youth movement. In his much discussed *Posdata* (*The Other Mexico*, 1970) he takes specific events as his point of departure; but his handling of the raw material differs markedly from that of writers like Monsiváis or Elena Poniatowska. Time, space, and his penchant for intellectualizing (and poeticizing) work to rob his essay of the journalistic immediacy and the sense of intense commitment typical of more youthful, more radical writers. Thus Jorge Aguilar Mora, one of his most articulate younger critics, notes in his *La divina pareja* (The divine couple, 1978) that Tlatelolco was not a "metaphor," as Paz would have us view it, but a very real tragedy.[28] Paz's relegation of the violent events of 1968 to a mythic, timeless zone of identity with the Mexico of Aztec ritual sacrifice is for him simply another example of Paz's characteristic tendency to juxtapose "history" versus "myth" and to opt for the latter. Stated somewhat differently, Aguilar Mora finds that his former mentor's recourse to myth leads him to value the aesthetic, poetic realm over historical reality. This position leads in turn to Paz's essential detachment from real events: "his entire method has consisted of this . . . in placing himself outside the historical whirlwind, because what annoys him is that history is in fact a whirlwind that enunciates incomprehensible and painful vital propositions for a person who only wishes to make metaphors."[29] It should be noted that Aguilar Mora's critique of Paz is not limited to comments on *Posdata*; indeed, Aguilar finds the same unacceptable tendencies in most of Paz's work, with the exception of his essays on poetry and aesthetics. Yet it is significant that the writings following Tlatelolco should elicit some of the sharpest attacks: clearly Paz's detachment, preoccupation with style, and distancing— elements which some feel are essential to the creation of genuinely literary essays—become suspect when violent events seem to demand authorial immediacy if not outrage. This interesting issue cannot be pursued here: raising it simply underscores the fact that 1968 was a watershed year and that the way writers reacted to its events helps define the generation under discussion.

Rebellion against a political force and its supporting establishment—in the Mexican case, against the PRI and the arbitrary, bureaucratic regime it perpetuated—is, however, only one dimension of the restiveness apparent during this period. On various levels and shaped by differing historical settings, a broadly felt revolutionary undercurrent or "wave" (again the term *onda* has also been used in this sense) is apparent in the work of leading essayists throughout the hemisphere. The essence of this phenomenon may be best described as a desire to break out of the social and spiritual restraints which remained from a more traditional, more prescriptive past. It takes many forms: the demand for sweeping social change, the cult of *el hombre nuevo* (a vaguely utopian notion current in the literature of heterodox Marxists, and others, since the mid-century), and especially the worldwide movement toward sexual liberation along with changed relations between the sexes.

The linkages between political, social, and economic realities and individual rebellion are complex. For a writer such as Julio Cortázar the attempts of creative people in Latin America to liberate themselves on a personal or professional level are doomed to failure since they are constrained by their "colonial" status, their dependent relationship to the materially richer and culturally more powerful nations of the developed world. This situation is, he feels, especially well illustrated with regard to erotic art. Thus, in his provocative essay "/que sepa abrir la puerta para ir a jugar" (/who knows how to open the door to go out to play), in his collagelike *Ultimo round*, he states that before the continent's writers can produce genuine erotic literature "it is necessary to conquer other liberties: colonization, poverty, and militarism also mutilate us aesthetically; to attempt the mastery of erotic language when political sovereignty has not even been achieved is an illusion of an adolescent who during his siesta leafs through a copy of *Playboy* with his one free hand . . . Will what we call erotic language even be *necessary* when literature is finally able to transmit any experience, even the most indescribable, without falling into the hands of municipal league of literary decency types?" (*UR*, 143). But exactly why does Latin America's undeveloped, "colonial," or dependent status impose this kind of restraint? Cortázar's answer seems to be that the area's creative people, its writers especially, feel somewhat like children when confronted by their European or North American confreres (perceived symbolically as schoolmaster authoritarian figures), who might reprimand them for being naughty. In simplest terms, Latin America suffers from a kind of insecurity or inferiority complex, which, though it has its roots in political and economic subordination, prevents the full development, or liberation, of its culture.

As we have seen, Mexico's Carlos Monsiváis, in analyzing his nation's desire for political and social change, focuses squarely on the youthful rebels of the 1960s and early 1970s who sought to achieve their objectives through rock music and drugs as well as by more usual means of protest. An important aspect of their rebellion involved their rejection of traditional sexual mores. Monsiváis, never solemn and very close to the movement he describes, treats this issue with considerable verve. His recounting of an interview with one of the charmingly brainless teenagers who enjoyed the Avándaro festival (the "Mexican Woodstock" of the early 1970s) completely naked is one of the high points of his book *Amor perdido*. While he apparently is sympathetically amused by such goings-on, true to a long tradition among essayists, he is quite capable of seeing both sides of the coin. Thus his positive attitude toward La Onda is undercut by serious doubts. Chief among these is that in the Mexican manifestation of the movement there was much false posturing, much playacting by bored middle-class kids who were simply copying another exotic fad. Not surprisingly, these reservations seem more apparent in Monsiváis's writing of the seventies, after La Onda had run its course; hence his comments on the Avándaro festival are to a considerable extent negative: "with regard to the search for alternatives [Avándaro] is a confirmation of dependency. Avándaro is an original and autonomous response, but it is also a colonial matter, not because a rock festival is exclusively North American, but rather because of its basic message: the unperturbed duplication of another's experience: that is to say, once again being up to date by dint of servile imitation."[30]

Similarly, in his lively discussion of the sex queen of Mexican films, Irma Serrano, or of the popular stripper Isela Vega (subtitled "On the New Status of Dirty Words") Monsiváis probes questions of changing mores, sexual revolution, censorship, and censureship with his characteristic mix of zany humor and serious concern. In both pieces he finds that beneath the superficial manifestations of the new sexuality lie frustration, boredom, and an essentially rebellious spirit. This is seen especially in the increasingly strong language that has come to characterize political rhetoric, social intercourse, and, obviously, the world of entertainment: "strong language aspires to the characteristics of a public challenge, a slap in the face of the System" (*AP*, 343). In a tone suggestive of Cortázar's essay, Monsiváis notes that a deep underlying cause of his nation's often pathetic attempts to change its traditional society may well be due to "a conditioned reflex of dependency" (*AP*, 297). And, again recalling Cortázar's line of thought, he urges his compatriots to abandon their childish modesty, their "well-mannered tone and . . . their ankle-length mental skirt," to be less subservient at international meetings, to say aloud " 'what the fuck' a thousand and one times without . . . feeling embarrassment, without expecting looks of disapproval" (*AP*, 320).

It is of some significance that Cortázar, an Argentine who attempted to write more explicitly erotic texts than most of his countrymen, left his homeland as a young man to spend the rest of his life in France. The fact is that Argentina, despite its claims of sophistication and cosmopolitanism, is not unlike many of its Spanish American neighbors in that emphasis on social propriety, including sexual repression, has always been a defining characteristic of its culture even until the very recent past. We have already noted that the Argentine essay, at least overtly, reveals little of the rebellion and turmoil found in other countries. Yet those writers who remained in Argentina from the 1960s through the early 1980s—Julio Mafud, Juan José Sebreli, Ernesto Sábato, among others—help us understand how recent Argentine history, as well as long-standing social constants, have shaped and at times repressed the mood of rebelliousness characteristic of Latin America during the period.

It would be difficult to underestimate the importance Perón and Peronism have played in all aspects of Argentine life since the mid-century. The full ramifications of this political—and social—movement cannot be treated here. Suffice it to say that the nation, after the regime of 1946 to 1955, was never quite the same: the long shadow of Perón and Peronism is especially evident in the expository prose of the 1960s and 1970s. Julio Mafud, one of Ezéquiel Martínez Estrada's "disciples" and the author of several rambling volumes that lie somewhere between pop-sociology and genuine essays, states unequivocally in his *Sociología del peronismo* (The sociology of Peronism, 1972) that "Peronism is for us the fundamental touchstone." He then notes that it led directly to much greater social mobility, to generational conflict, and to sexual confrontation.[31] Mafud's attitudes to changes in Argentine society of the post-Perón period seem, however, to be quite ambiguous. In an earlier essay, *Los argentinos y el status* (Argentineans and status, 1969), he is critical of the new pattern of family relationships, especially of permissive parents who cater to the whims of their children, and he is disturbed by the increasing emphasis on consumerism and material wealth. To what extent these phenomena are products of the Perón years is never fully clarified. Although Peronism, with its populist *justicialismo* appeal, was hardly a genuine revolutionary movement, it clearly served as a catalyst for social change. It gave the lower classes a stronger voice, and in part through the efforts of Eva Perón it accelerated the Argentine women's movement. These issues become murky when the question of motives is considered. Was Eva simply being the dutiful wife helping her husband manipulate the country's masses, or did she have a genuine feminist agenda? At any rate, Mafud would have us believe that a "new Argentine woman" emerges in the post-Perón period. He notes this phenomenon and the accompanying changes in relations between the sexes in another of his many essays, *Psicología de la viveza criolla* (Psychology of our native astuteness, 1965, 1973).[32] In one chapter of this volume, "Prologue to Liberation," he describes women in the workplace who wear pants and who no longer are the easy targets of male sexist remarks. In another essay (and a bit of a potboiler), *La revolución sexual argentina* (The Argentinean sexual revolution, 1966), he seems to fear the "masculinization" of women, unisex clothing, and the growing use of strong language among certain contemporary writers.[33]

Juan José Sebreli, a heterodox Marxist, a one-time supporter of Perón, and another prolific essayist, has investigated questions of feminism, the sexual revolution, the role of Eva Perón, and related issues in several book-length studies. In his *Eva Perón, ¿aventurera o militante?* (Eva Perón: Adventuress or militant? 1969), a work dedicated to Simone de Beauvoir and prefaced by an epigraph from Sartre stressing the role of the individual in history, he appears quite sympathetic to the attractive actress who rose from obscurity and illegitimacy to become the first lady of Argentina. The most interesting discussion in this essay is found in his interpretation of Evita as a classic "outsider," an illegitimate child whose support of the marginalized sectors of Argentine society constituted a threat to the establishment and so infused a revolutionary spirit into Peronism.[34] Sebreli thus links the sexual revolution, as epitomized in this more "clitoral" than "vaginal" woman (*EP*, 77), with a much broader sociopolitical movement. The basic question—whether Eva was a genuine militant or a mere opportunist—is left unanswered. Viewed historically, he feels, the fact that she contributed to the partial emancipation of women and to the melioration of the working class makes the question immaterial (*EP*, 90).

An examination of these and other essays of Sebreli suggests that any latent rebelliousness in Argentine society during the 1960s and 1970s remained essentially beneath the surface despite the Peronist legacy of restiveness. Thus terms such as "alienation" and "repression" figure prominently in a series of essays describing the period: *Buenos Aires, vida cotidiana y alienación* (Buenos Aires, daily life and alienation, 1965), *Mar del Plata: el ocio represivo* (Mar del Plata: Repressive leisure, 1970), and *Fútbol y masas* (Soccer and the masses, 1981) all point in this direction. In the first of these, for example, he paints a dreary picture of the urban middle class. Basically conformist, given to the soporific cult of *telenovelas*, sports, and creature comforts and subject to a hypocritical code of sexual conventionality (which incidentally includes masturbation), their lives are passed in boring housing developments, in gastro-centric activities, and in an essential resistance to anything new.[35] Moreover, much of the youth—the traditional catalysts of rebellion—have become consumer-oriented fops, not unlike London's "Teddy boys" of the period (*BA*, 101). Toward the conclusion of *Buenos Aires, vida cotidiana y alienación* he notes that although the "whirlwind of uncontrolled Peronist adventure" disturbed the lower and middle classes deeply, its revolutionary message was stillborn: the working class, just beginning to enjoy a somewhat better life, pathetically looked only toward the middle class as a model. Most important, the Argentine left was completely incapable of reaching the masses—of transforming their frustration into genuine revolutionary activity (*BA*, 187). Sebreli concludes on a somewhat abstract note of hopeful optimism: "today's daily existence with its banality, bad faith, wretchedness, and failure can become a life of generosity, authenticity, joy, and lucidity when man, by becoming aware of his alienation, frees himself of his servitude to inhuman idols and by his active shaping of his world will no longer fatalistically accept suffering" (*BA*, 189).

A less sanguine tone dominates his tellingly titled *Mar del Plata: el ocio represivo*, a nostalgic essay that recalls the past and present of Argentina's most popular seaside resort. The basic theme here is that the middle class's traditional vacation of a week or two by the sea is a snare and delusion. Throughout the year, he notes, people work hard, live dull lives pathetically looking forward to something different—to a carnivalesque period when all rules of propriety are relaxed, when they may return to an almost mythical belle epoque; but inevitably the reality of vacation is something much more prosaic. Commercial interests and local municipal authorities contrive to produce a synthetic environment designed simply to manipulate vacationers for profit. Interestingly, Sebreli holds that an important element in the "bait" to attract the clientele is sex: in effect, the manipulators try to infuse the general atmosphere of Mar del Plata with a vague promise of erotic adventure. In reality male vacationers (and presumably male hotel workers, who consider sexual conquests a kind of fringe benefit of their seasonal employment) end up carrying on sordid affairs with the many "summer widows" or with prostitutes.[36] And for the teenagers, Sebreli slyly observes, there are always the charms of furtive moments in the back seat of the family car or of voyeurism through the gaps of the boardwalk accompanied by masturbation (*MP*, 60). What Sebreli appears to condemn most vehemently is the fact that free, open sexuality is not tolerated: Mar del Plata's beaches are policed at night and few if any hotels knowingly accept unmarried couples. Quick to see political overtones in any situation, Sebreli observes that "authoritarians and prejudiced people like Onganía" (*MP*, 129) would consider such tolerance a threat to social and political order.[37] Thus titillation and covert sexual activity are tolerated, if not encouraged, but the manipulation and commercialization of eros serve to defuse its essentially revolutionary character: "love has ceased to be a free activity and has been converted into a factory product, to be consumed, [thus] losing its anarchic freedom . . . it becomes converted, like leisure, into an activity . . . controlled by society. Desires that used to be simply repressed are channeled toward the interests of the consumer society. Mar del Plata is, in this respect, a typical example" (*MP*, 129).

In a later essay, *Fútbol y masas*, Sebreli follows a similar trajectory but with specific reference to sports. Like its manipulation of sexuality, the establishment directly or indirectly uses large-scale sporting events (chiefly "major league" soccer in the Argentine context) to control and "depoliticize" the masses.[38] Taking his cue from noted German critic Theodor Adorno, he equates sports with fascism and other repressive antilibertarian forces. Sebreli maintains that the cult of sports not only "depoliticizes" but, even worse, encourages violence and aggression—not against the authority of the state, one infers, but against the weaker elements of society. In short, he comes very close to saying (though he never quite explains the connection) that the cult of sports supports and abets violent authoritarian regimes such as those headed by Argentina's military dictators of the 1960s and 1970s (*FM*, 121). Moreover, he finds it incomprehensible that fellow intellectuals on the left such as Ernesto Sábato or Eduardo Galeano have written sympathetically about modern mass sports (*FM*, 142–143).[39] Like many independent Latin American Marxists of recent decades, Sebreli does not limit his condemnation to the West. Thus he finds a similar manipulative use of sport among the Soviets (*FM*, 180–181) and concludes that the masses of both East and West prefer "the sanctimonious veneration of the populists to the harsh criticism of those who try to help [the masses] raise their own consciousness" (*FM*, 182).

The desire of many intellectuals—especially those whom we might consider heterodox Marxists—to make the masses "raise their consciousness" is closely related to a concept to which I have already made brief reference, that of *el hombre nuevo*—the "New Man." By the 1960s this term had become almost a catchword among many Spanish American writers representing a broad ideological spectrum. It even appears in the folksongs and popular literature of the period. While it suggests different things to different people, it is clearly related to the broad issues surrounding revolution and rebellion. Perhaps the central idea (and it is hardly a novelty) is that a new ethic or new spirit must accompany or precede political and economic change. An essay such as Julio Mafud's *El hombre nuevo: liberación y revolución* (The new man: Liberation and revolution, 1973) attempts to address these matters directly, but with only limited success. In this work the notion of the *hombre nuevo* is never really defined, though we do learn something of its genesis among certain non-Hispanic thinkers. Among these Franz Fanon and Herbert Marcuse figure prominently: the latter's concept of the "total man," as opposed to "unidimensional man," seems especially important. Thus Mafud criticizes the Soviets, who, he feels, have sacrificed genuine "socialist morality" for an "industrial" morality. By contrast, he sees a genuine, existential model of the *hombre nuevo* in the person of Che Guevara.[40] Mafud, however, is not an especially original or consistent thinker. His essay works toward a rather typical simplistic exhortation for leftists to press for "national liberation" rather than a classical revolution, since the presence of fully evolved capitalism along with imperialism in Latin America makes a European-type revolution virtually impossible. Citing Che Guevara again he calls for "two . . . three . . . many Vietnams" (*HN*, 137). However, at the very end of his text he returns, somewhat awkwardly, to the *hombre nuevo* theme when he states that "moral education" is a prerequisite for genuine liberation and that the development of a superior ethic is the only way to prevent the corruption inherent in any revolution. In short, *El hombre nuevo* is little more than a verbose exercise in leftist rhetoric that leaves Mafud's position ill-defined. Is he calling for a military uprising aimed at national liberation or simply an educational campaign? Does his enthusiastic praise of Che Guevara imply support for Castro's Cuba or does he see Fidel and Che as antagonists? And finally, what bearing has all this upon the realities of his own nation, Argentina?

In one way or another the notion of the *hombre nuevo*, broadly conceived, can be seen just below the surface in the essays of such diverse writers as Ernesto Sábato, Eduardo Galeano, Octavio Paz, Julio Cortázar, and others. His presence may also be sensed in the writings of several figures on the periphery of the Spanish American essay. I am thinking here of certain religious dissenters of the left, people close to the liberation theology movement[41] such as Colombian revolutionary priest Camilo Torres and Sandinista radical poet Ernesto Cardenal. The latter's essay "Un marxismo con San Juan de la Cruz" (A Marxism with St. John of the Cross) reveals an interesting blend of guerrilla/true believer who constitutes a kind of *hombre nuevo* whose "primary task" as a Christian is to work for revolution.[42] Even Ernesto Sábato, whose position is considerably removed from the militancy of Camilo Torres or Ernesto Cardenal, has frequently revealed that his vision of the *hombre nuevo* is colored by strong religious convictions. The Argentine essayist, influenced by the "personalist" thinking of C. Mounier (a priest and an important figure in the left wing of French Catholicism), has often stressed the spiritual component in contemporary radical movements and their leaders. For example, in his 1967 "Homenaje a Ernesto Guevara" (Homage to Ernesto Guevara) he states: "for me and I believe for many, in effect for millions of men . . . he [Guevara] died for an ideal infinitely more praiseworthy than the material improvement of the poor . . . he died for the ideal of the New Man."[43] In sum, the *hombre nuevo* may be a guerrilla fighting for a cause with religious fervor or little more than a flower child who professes rebellion; he may even be the protesting student who, as Cortázar records, wrote, "The more I make love the more I want to make revolution."

Though he does not attempt to define the *hombre nuevo*, in his essayistic mélange of memoirs, confessions, observations, and musings, *Días y noches de amor y guerra*, Eduardo Galeano presents a revealing self-portrait of the Latin American *hombre nuevo* of the 1960s and 1970s. As a young exile from the repressive military dictatorship of his native Uruguay and as a struggling writer, he mingles with students, poor *campesinos*, and urban slum dwellers. Though his life is not easy he recounts in this book many pleasurable, even poetic moments. He intersperses ironic, often biting, criticism of society (in the sections titled "The System," for example) with autobiographical detail, frequently intimate in nature. A good example of this blend of material may be seen in a fragment titled "Quito, marzo de 1976: última noche" (Quito, March of 1976: The last night).

> The telephone rings. It is time to leave. We have not slept more than a few minutes but we feel fresh and wide awake.
>
> We have been making love and have been eating and drinking, with the sheet as our tablecloth and our legs as a kind of table and we've again been making love.
>
> She's told me about troubles in Chile. It seems difficult, she tells me, that her comrades are dead, after having seen them so very alive. She just barely escaped and now she wonders what to do with so much freedom and such an excess of life.
>
> We arrive late at the airport. The plane leaves behind schedule. We have breakfast three times.
>
> We have known each other for half a day.
>
> I walk, without turning around, toward the plane. The field is surrounded by blue volcanos. I sense surprise at the electricity and hunger of my body. (*DN*, 130)

The Hispanic *hombre nuevo* is then a rebel who combines political activism (usually, but not always, within some kind of leftist frame) with either a sense of achieved personal liberation or a desire for such liberation. Often, moreover, his underlying animus is infused with a vaguely defined religiosity, and since he is opposed to "the system," frequently this opposition takes the form of seeking sexual liberation.

Readers sensitive to current concerns regarding sexism in literature and "phallocentric" writing will no doubt question the repeated use of the masculine form *hombre nuevo* by the essayists just discussed. In effect, the entire matter of sexual revolution, changing sex roles, and related issues has, in the Spanish American context, been dominated—with only a few exceptions—by male writers who more often than not reveal a classical sexist viewpoint. This situation has not gone unnoticed; for example, one North American critic,

Martha Paley Francescato, has focused squarely on this question in a perceptive critique of Cortázar in an article "The New Man (But not the New Woman)." These concerns lead to a related but broader issue: that of the role of women essayists during the period under consideration. One might suppose if anyone would articulate the position of women with regard to the social and political ferment pervading Latin America during the late 1960s and 1970s it would be women themselves, and indeed several figures come to mind, including a few writers of essays.

One such person would certainly be Argentina's Victoria Ocampo (1890–1979). The director of *Sur*, South America's most prestigious literary magazine for many years and a sophisticated polygraph, Ocampo has left a substantial corpus of writing on women's issues as well as many impressive essays on literature, politics, cultural relations, and the like.[44] However, the fact that by our period she was well over seventy and had made her major contributions during the middle decades of the century places her outside the scope of this study.

A better case can be made for Rosario Castellanos (1925–1974) of Mexico. Known primarily as an accomplished writer of prose fiction, Castellanos nonetheless produced a number of fine texts—newspaper reportage, but legitimate essays in my view—that reveal keen insight into many of the questions under discussion here. Some of her best essayistic pieces are collected in a volume covering her work from the early 1960s until her untimely death in 1974, *El uso de la palabra* (The use of words, 1988). The first section of this volume, "Cosas de mujeres" (Women's things), is especially rich in material relative to social change and the women's movement. In a comment of 1970, for example, she notes the activities of feminists in the United States—their protest marches, their symbolic strike against performing routine domestic duties, and their campaign against magazines that exploit women as sex objects.[45] While she applauds these initiatives by her North American sisters she notes that relatively few Mexicans have also voiced approval. Castellanos's comment on the Mexican attitude in this regard is intriguing: "everyone refers to this movement of women's liberation in the United States as if it were occurring in the most remote country of the world or on an unexplored planet. It is as if what were happening on the other side of the Río Grande did not concern us at all" (*UP*, 50). She goes on to note that this attitude would be understandable if one were dealing with typically North American problems such as race or Vietnam, but not regarding women. She concludes the essay by noting that Mexican women—who, she feels, are more "parasites" than "victims" in present-day society—may actually enjoy their dubious status. However, times are changing; when women have to work in factories or offices and also must take care of the home, when the accelerating development of Mexico makes the institution of the domestic maid disappear, characterized as that "cosy mattress upon which our conformity reposes," only then "will the first furious female rebel appear" (*UP*, 52). Before taking leave of Castellanos, it should be noted again that this theme—her thoughts on the eventual emergence of a genuine Latin American *mujer nueva*—is only one of her many concerns. Politics, Mexico's image abroad, and literary questions all surface in her sparse but very perceptive essays.

Even among writers who shun the term *hombre nuevo* and attack those who glorify the concept, some form of sexual revisionism is often regarded as one of the desiderata of a better society. Octavio Paz, for example, has frequently set forth a utopian vision of a society free of the inhibitions and hypocrisy inherent in contemporary sexual mores. Indeed, the relationship between physical love and Paz's very personal concept of revolution is one of the constants in his thinking. It is easy to find abundant support for this in his first major essay, *El laberinto de soledad* (*The Labyrinth of Solitude*, 1950, 1959) and even earlier.[46] For Paz the act of love puts men and women (his stress on mutuality of desire places him apart from many of Spanish America's more phallocentric writers) in contact with their authentic being and as such it constitutes a liberation from the alienating forces of society and its institutions. Thus, "everything is opposed to it: morality, classes, laws, races." Perhaps his strongest statement in this regard is found toward the conclusion of this celebrated essay: "to defend love has always been a dangerous antisocial activity. And now it begins to be truly revolutionary."[47] Paz's special sensitivity toward these issues obviously antedates the "sexual revolution" by many years—his readings of André Breton and the French surrealists, who were thinking along these lines in the 1920s and 1930s, probably accounts for his attitudes in this regard.

In his essays of recent decades Paz has continued to explore these themes but with a significantly different emphasis. His guide in texts such as *Los hijos del limo* (*Children of the Mire*, 1974) and *El ogro filantrópico* (The philanthropic ogre, 1979) is frequently Charles Fourier, the early nineteenth-century utopian who envisaged a communal society characterized by material abundance and erotic freedom and who saw the source of social relations in the "passionate attraction" of sexuality. Paz's brilliant essay on "La mesa y el lecho" (The table and the bed), included in *El ogro*, was written in Cambridge, Massachusetts, in 1971: its sources lie not only in Fourier's writings[48] but in Paz's experience in the United States. The essay is structured around a comparison of Fourier's utopia, "Harmonia," with "civilization" as exemplified by contemporary North America. Paz focuses on the "legislation of pleasure" as a basic theme and, within this category, upon the pleasures of the bed and the table. This seemingly idiosyncratic approach is drawn from Fourier's utopia, where "Religion" is in charge of all things pleasurable, especially sex and gastronomy. Unlike modern "civilization," where religious (and presumably other repressive) institutions control, suppress, or shunt pleasure aside, in Fourier's ideal society "religion no longer oppresses but rather it liberates, exalts and harmonizes the instincts, without excluding any of them" (*OF*, 214). Paz's comments on North American society of the period—our gastronomic as well as sexual preferences—are somewhat ambiguous despite his generally sympathetic appreciation of this nation. He believes that the United States's puritanical values of work, savings, and accumulation still dominate and that pleasure is frequently seen in terms of a "wasteful" activity. However, he notes that in North American society of the late 1960s "this word [pleasure] is now coming forth with violent vehemence" (*OF*, 221); a portent, he feels, of a change in the course of our society. Yet he concludes that the chances for any profound, truly revolutionary changes in North American society still remain remote, as they are elsewhere, since there no longer exists (and by this point Paz is considering the question in worldwide perspective) a proletariat with a genuine revolutionary vocation. If any change is to come about, he holds, it will not be along the lines of classical Marxist revolution, but rather it could be "an immense mutation, perhaps more profound than revolution . . . whose consequences are as of now impossible to predict" (*OF*, 221).

In sum, Paz foresees the possibility of a different kind of revolution—a "mutation," as he puts it—that has as its goal the liberation of humanity from "civilized" society's denial of pleasure, sexual or otherwise. While it is doubtful that he envisions anything quite like a literal implementation of Fourier's "Harmonia," he does feel that a recognition of desire, of "passionate attraction," can contribute to a better future society. Not surprisingly, he finds few indications that this change will come about in the Marxist world: "in the communist countries there is no erotic rebellion and, as we all know, the price of sexual deviations is prison and the forced labor camp" (*OF*, 234). This irrefutable statement (made, it should be remembered, in the late 1970s) raises some interesting questions, especially for Latin America's left. Despite the recurring notion of the *hombre nuevo* as a sexually liberated, militant revolutionary (recall again Galeano's self-image, Monsiváis's naked flower children playing at revolution at the Avándaro festival, or Cortázar's sympathetic documentation of the sexually charged student rebels of 1968), the social and political realities of Marxist regimes are in sharp contrast with what Latin American and other Western radicals have stressed in their vision of sociopolitical melioration. As for Paz, toward the end of his complex essay, he confirms this view when he points out that "the rebellion against repressive morality is tied to two conditions that, if they do not determine it, at least explain it: economic abundance and political democracy." Paz concludes that the erotic rebellion is "a symptom of a decisive fact that is destined to alter the course of North American history and that of the entire world: the downfall of Protestant capitalism's value system" (*OF*, 234). Since he obviously cannot envision the Marxist world bringing about any genuine change and in view of the fact that he finds the future of "Protestant capitalism's value system" in doubt, one wonders exactly what Paz sees on humanity's distant horizon.

The themes that have concerned us in this chapter—revolution, rebellion, the youth movement, the *hombre nuevo*, "liberation" in various senses, but especially with regard to human sexuality—reflect a society that was undergoing rapid and perhaps profound changes. The widespread restiveness that characterizes all these phenomena has been a major rallying point in the left's appeal. But a number of essayists of widely differing approaches and of widely varying literary talent begin to undermine the left's one-time monopoly of revolutionary rhetoric. A former Peronist and heterodox Marxist like Juan José Sebreli, an unabashed defender of free enterprise and the North American political system such as Carlos Rangel, or a poet-essayist with a romantic vision of the future like Octavio Paz offers Latin Americans alternative explanations and—in the context of the prevailing ideas of the early years of the period under discussion—genuine voices of dissent.

The Cult of Pepsicoátl

THREE

"Children are by nature ungrateful . . . they come home from school, they press a button, sit down to watch their favorite TV program without even thinking for a moment about the technological marvel that television represents. Therefore it would not be amiss to recount for the younger generation the history of scientific progress . . . to demonstrate the admirable results of human effort." So begins the pompous, cliché-ridden authorial voice in Julio Cortázar's sly mini-essay "El tesoro de la juventud" (The treasure of youth). He goes on to praise the qualities of the modern supersonic jet but soon notes that "science is pre-eminently an endless search and thus jets have been superceded by new and more impressive examples of human ingenuity," namely propeller-driven aircraft, "since flying at lower speed and altitude the pilot has a greater advantage in maintaining a steady course and in safely executing take-off and landing procedures." Nevertheless, he continues, "technologists, ever searching for newer and superior means of communication, after a while came up with two capital inventions: we refer to steamships and railroads. For the first time, thanks to these, the extraordinary conquest of travel on the surface of the earth—with the undeniable safety margin that it represents—was achieved." A parallel discussion of "progress" in maritime transportation follows: not surprisingly, this takes the form of moving from modern ships to sailboats, to paddling one's own canoe and so on. The "crowning achievement of the scientific pyramid" is, of course, walking and swimming: thus the essay concludes, "perhaps this is the reason that there are so many people on the beaches, since technology's progress, though many youngsters are unaware of it, ends up by being acclaimed by all humanity—especially during vacation time" (*UR*, pb, 28). Trivial, perhaps even silly, Cortázar's text nonetheless points up a growing concern: namely, that technological progress cannot be taken at face value. What may appear to bring about greater material comfort, improved conditions, or better communications may in fact have negative consequences. In short, the entire issue of technology and progress is debatable. Also contributing to the total impact of the text is the authorial voice in which this message is couched—that of a manipulative, authoritarian member of the establishment lecturing young people. The suggestion here is, of course, that the powers that be have been using the unquestioned cult of progress to further enhance their position.

Put into the context of contemporary Spanish America the debate surrounding progress and technology becomes especially intense. In the first place technological advances cannot be considered in isolation from a wide range of complex accompanying phenomena: demographic shifts, political changes, along with important modifications in attitudes and values. In short, we are faced with the broad process of "development" as social scientists have come to use this term since the mid-century. Second, for most Latin Americans, technology and development—both as processes and as mind-sets—are understandably equated with foreign influence. With only minor exceptions manufactured goods as well as many cultural artifacts (especially films, TV programs, and popular music) come from the United States, Europe, or Japan. Their presence in the practical sense of goods to be paid for or as signs of foreign cultural incursions has traditionally provided thinkers of widely varying ideological persuasions with a rallying ground from which to defend the nation and at times "Latin culture."[1] Third, while many Latin American writers have expressed strong reservations with regard to developmental thinking and blind faith in progress, it is difficult to deny the genuine need to resolve the region's practical problems in areas such as agriculture, health, and housing. Finally, like people everywhere, Spanish Americans have become aware of the dark side of modern technology: ecological damage, pollution, and a pervasive dehumanization transcending political and ideological boundaries.

A fundamental question underlying the discussions surrounding technology, progress, and development involves the basic relationship of Latin America toward the rest of the world. The continent's "peripheral" or "marginal" status with respect to Europe and North America has been a genuinely classical theme among its thinkers. Essayists such as Ezéquiel Martínez Estrada, Alfonso Reyes, and the early Octavio Paz were acutely aware of it during the 1940s and 1950s: indeed, these concerns have clear antecedents in the work of Rodó and others writing at the turn of the century. However, with the emergence of the postwar world, the demise of colonialism in Asia and Africa, and the polarization created by the Cold War, the question of Latin America's relationship to other—especially the more developed—areas called for fresh perspectives and new formulations. For some these needs were met by the notion that Latin America formed part of the "Third World," a term that since the 1950s had been gaining favor internationally among economists, political scientists, and statesmen.

It is not my purpose to assess the validity of this concept, yet it seems fair to say that since its inception it has been flexibly, if not ill, defined. Some—including a number of our essayists—would hold that as applied to Spanish America it is at best imprecise and at worst pernicious. Much of the confusion regarding the term stems, it seems, from the fact that in the period of its genesis the determinants of the concept were, on the one hand, political ("Third World" meant any nation not aligned with either the Soviets or the Americans) or, on the other, economic ("Third World" meant any country that was poor or underdeveloped, with respect to the wealthy industrial nations). Obviously, these two ways of defining the Third World do not coincide in all cases; likewise, some writers approach the concept primarily in terms of international politics while others work on the premise that "underdevelopment" and "Third World" are virtually synonymous.

Argentine J. J. Sebreli, in his essay *Tercer mundo, mito burgués* (The third world, a bourgeois myth, 1975), illustrates quite nicely the complexity of *tercermundismo* (Third Worldism) and how the notion can become embroiled in ideological polemics. The provocative title gives a good indication of Sebreli's point of view, and at the conclusion of his introductory chapter he enlarges upon his basic position: "We propose . . . to show that contrary to the opinion of the *tercermundistas*, the revolutionary struggle is one and the same throughout the world, since the real conditions for the solidarity of the oppressed in the first, second, and third worlds [do] exist . . . Imperialism has not cut the world into three parts—as the *tercermundistas* hold—on the contrary the international market has made the world an indivisible whole . . . There is no longer any room for the anarchy of fascism or for the 'socialism in one country' of Stalinism."[2] Beneath the surface of this somewhat abstract pronouncement can be seen the views of a theoretical Marxist—not untouched by Trotskyite polemics—who is reacting sharply against the leftist nationalism so typical of Argentine and other Latin American radical thought. A bit later he attacks those who use national character or cultural determinants to distinguish Third World countries from others (*TMM*, 58–59). Throughout he stresses classical, "pure" Marxist formulations to refute the ideas and praxis of leftists, be they radical Peronists, mainstream Argentine communists, or confused *tercermundistas* who mistakenly believe themselves Marxists.

The core of Sebreli's argument is that Third World thinking, which typically relies upon simplistic "dependency theory" (we are poor because they, the developed nations, are rich), fails to see the process in orthodox Marxist terms. How this position bears upon the question of development is one of the most interesting facets of his argument. Imperialism, he claims, "does not bring on underdevelopment but rather a deformed, one-sided development. That a country can have a high level of development and still be subject to imperialism is glaringly demonstrated by the cases of . . . Finland, Australia . . . Canada, Brazil, Mexico, and Argentina itself. By contrast countries truly underdeveloped are precisely those that have been deprived of all contact with imperialistic powers, for example, Afghanistan . . . Nepal . . . and Yemen" (*TMM*, 160). While Sebreli does not claim that the development of poorer nations by the industrial powers is beneficial to all classes in the less developed country (the middle class tends to gain more than the masses), he does view the process positively and as one consistent with classical Marxist analysis. Earlier in his essay he points out Marx's well-known tenet that the growth and power of the bourgeoisie was a necessary step in the revolutionary process; a point, he feels, frequently disregarded by contemporary leftists and especially by ardent *tercermundistas* (*TMM*, 152). Genuine development, then, can only come about by following strictly interpreted Marxist theory.

Countries that attempt development through unorthodox short cuts (what Sebreli calls *sustituísmo*, that is, "substitutionism") are, he maintains, doomed to rule by repressive, bureaucratic dictatorships. His prime example here is Cuba, whom he attacks mercilessly (*TMM*, 223–225). Although he can appreciate the historical role of capitalism and the bourgeoisie as part of the process toward revolution, he realizes that the Third World cannot turn back the clock to the conditions of classical free enterprise; moreover, the modern bourgeoisie of Latin America "are incapable of playing the same role that in their day the English, French or North American bourgeoisie played" (*TMM*, 238). Given these doubts concerning the role of the middle class and of free enterprise capitalism in furthering genuine development and considering his rejection of the "hell of bureaucratic dictatorship" (*TMM*, 235) as epitomized by the former Soviet Union or Castro's Cuba, what course can Latin America—and presumably the rest of the Third World—follow? "There exists only one alternative to this depressing panorama and it is the fall of capitalism in the advanced countries and the fall of bureaucracy in the collectivist regimes. This would permit fraternal help to backward countries that would not mean a new form of oppression" (*TMM*, 235). This rather fuzzy utopian scenario seems quite unlikely, despite the recent demise of Eastern European regimes. At any rate, what should Latin America do while waiting for the millennium or to hasten its coming? Sebreli suggests that only the "Marxist premise" can serve as a guide; that the "revolutionary evolution" would involve "an implacable struggle on one front against all forms of *sustituísmo*—that is, abandoning the revolutionary task to small conspiratorial elites who would bring about revolution instead of the working class—and, on the other front, against the symmetrically opposite error of 'massism' " (*TMM*, 240). The latter term is clarified to some extent in a more recent text, his article "No caer en la adoración de las masas" (Do not give way to worshiping the masses, 1980). In this essay he again stresses the point that according to Marx "socialism is only possible in those societies where capitalism has achieved the greatest development of productive forces. Socialism means the dividing up of wealth, for which reason it is inconceivable in a backward country where the only thing that can be divided up is poverty."[3] In the same piece he attacks the extreme left, especially in Argentina, for considering democracy to be a "deception" and merely "bourgeois formalism." He also criticizes the left for not admitting that the nation's workers have little or no interest in revolution, for not conceding that a functioning democracy "is the most adequate space in which to fight for socialism," and, finally, for believing that all movements supported by the masses—Peronism, for example—are unerringly progressive. He even cites Marx and Engels on the point that the two founders of socialism on occasion would not hesitate to characterize the masses as "stupid" and "infantile."[4]

On balance Sebreli's essay tends to be bookish and abstract. He avoids making many specific observations regarding Latin American reality, and unless the reader is fairly well acquainted with the fine points of Marxist argumentation, the text can become quite tedious. Practical matters, such as the nature of development, its limitations and dangers, the appropriateness of various kinds of technology, and so on are all sketchy. In a word Sebreli, at least in this book, is first and foremost an ideologue whose brief encounters with concrete reality are subordinated to a passionate interpretation of Marxism. Despite the essay's title, he appears more interested in a vague "revolutionary task" than he is in the Third World. Moreover, his distaste for virtually all forms of contemporary radicalism places him in a position quite isolated from most parties and regimes of either the left or right.

Carlos Rangel, the Venezuelan writer and journalist whom we met in the preceding chapter, provides in his essay *El tercermundismo* (Third Worldism, 1982) an interesting contrast to Sebreli's thinking. Though they are written from different viewpoints, the two books have some broad similarities. For example, it is fascinating to see how certain basic statements of Rangel, an avowed champion of North American–type capitalism, coincide with those of Sebreli, a devoted Marxist ideologue. Thus, early in his essay the Venezuelan asserts:

> not only the Leninist-Marxists but even the democratic socialists . . . are infected with the set idea that the advance of Socialism, where it can and should occur from now on, is in the poor and backward countries . . . Only in this way can we explain that . . . even the social democrats do not object but rather rejoice that the Russians and their Cuban delegates might take over, for example, the Nicaraguan revolution. . . . This attitude and complex of ideas, beliefs, and sentiments that support it is the *tercermundismo* in the title of this book, an ideology both confused and simplistic, but in spite of this (or because of it) it has become the most widespread component of the socialist spirit and serves as compensation for its failures and disillusionments in other areas.
>
> It is a matter that would have astounded the original socialist theoreticians and especially Marx and Engels, who would have rejected as barbarous and dangerous that there exists an affinity and predestined link between socialism and underdevelopment.[5]

Both Sebreli and Rangel are concerned with Latin America's relationship to the more developed, industrialized world, and both look upon the term "Third World" with considerable suspicion. Rangel, for his part, seldom uses the phrase without the modifier *llamado* (so-called). Most interesting, too, is the *apparent* similarity of their critique of the Third World's recourse to dependency theory. On close inspection, however, it can be seen that Rangel bases his views on tenets diametrically opposed to those of the Argentine. In the first place, Latin American intellectuals, Rangel feels, have been loathe to ascribe the continent's underdevelopment and related problems to internal causes; instead, they seek the source for backwardness in the dependency theory or similar explanations. Second, Marxism, the remedy for the continent's ills prescribed by a chorus of leftist thinkers, leads only to a repressive state, bureaucracy, and failed developmental goals. Unlike Sebreli, Rangel never suggests that a purer form of Marxism—one quite dissimilar from that observed in Cuba, China, or the Soviet Union—might lead to an ideal, utopian society. Finally, he holds that the free enterprise system, as exemplified in the Western democracies, notably the United States, provides the best model for the progress and development of the "so-called" Third World, of which he considers Latin America a part. These uncomplicated ideas underlie Rangel's *El tercer-*

mundismo and, as we saw, his earlier essay *Del buen salvaje al buen revolucionario.* Again, it must be noted that given the intellectual climate of the period, it is not surprising that Rangel should have been considered a maverick, a bête noire in the eyes of the academic community, or, in our terms, a very outspoken voice of dissent.

In the third chapter of *El tercermundismo* Rangel explores the basic idea of the term at greater length. As we have noted above, he considers Third Worldism to be the "most widespread component" of the socialist position as well as the "compensation" for Marxism's failures. He begins his exploration of the concept by tracing *tercermundismo*'s origins during the immediate postwar years when it presumably was applied to the neutral nations who were "nonaligned with respect to the Soviet-U.S. confrontation." From the outset, he maintains, the term was inaccurate since most of the nations (including those of Latin America) were more or less in the Western camp. However, by 1980, Rangel claims, this situation had reversed itself. With the "audacious military and diplomatic expansion" of the Russians much of the so-called Third World— Cuba, Central America, parts of the Middle East and Africa—had come under Soviet influence. Realizing that the classical Marxist position of revolution in the advanced industrial nations was not working out, communists the world over, he maintains, quickly shifted the terms of their analysis. The poor, backward countries, now viewed as the "proletariat," came to be seen as in conflict with the rich developed nations, now considered the "bourgeoisie." In short, the traditional class struggle was transformed into international political relationships. Since the proletariat in Marxist theory is by definition exploited, the poverty of the poor, backward nations—the Third World—is explained by the wealth of the developed world. Thus, the situation of the Third World is equated with what has been loosely termed the dependency theory. As Rangel puts it, "*Tercermundismo*, so stylish today, consists essentially . . . in the proposition that the backwardness of the underdeveloped countries as well as the progress of the developed countries . . . are due to imperialist exploration and the debilitating effect of dependency . . . Thus in this way one explains the fact that *tercermundismo* has literally been transformed into the passion of all those who hold to anticapitalist ideas and sentiments, not only in the Third World, but as well and even more so in the developed countries" (*T*, 74).

Rangel, of course, has carefully outlined this position only to attack it. He immediately states that this kind of thinking does not depend simply on a rational belief in current Marxist theory. Rather, many in the Third World have embraced it because of their irrational, almost pathological obsessions. These people "include all the discontented, all those who are frustrated, disoriented, all the losers, all those who are irrational," and, he adds, "those who for whatever reason reject or are afraid of the consequences of scientific and technological development, of industrialism and the growth of cities" (*T*, 74). This last point is significant with respect to the main themes of the present chapter: it is another indication that while Latin Americans in general envy the wealth and material progress of the advanced nations, many—including leftists and other "irrational" or "frustrated" elements, if we accept Rangel's characterization—have serious reservations regarding the benefits of development.

For Rangel, however, most of these fears are unfounded. His admiration for the free enterprise, industrialized world, especially the United States, knows no bounds. By contrast, the prevailing *malestar* (sickness) of the Third World, he feels, is "an ambivalent, almost schizophrenic attitude with regard to one's own culture . . . which leads inevitably to a painful feeling of inferiority, to self-disdain and even self-hatred" (*T*, 79). Rangel goes on to define the Third World as "those countries where lack of self-esteem and lack of faith in oneself, along with the consequent lack of confidence in development within the world capitalist system, incline people to accept, in either a diffuse or forthright way, the . . . thesis of imperialism and dependency as an explanation of their problems" (*T*, 79). At one point in his essay he further suggests that the growing fear of apocalyptic ecological doom is, at least in part, just another manifestation of the Third World's hatred of capitalism; that is, Latin Americans and other Third Worlders believe that pollution and environmental damage is primarily a product of capitalistic development (*T*, 185).

Toward the conclusion of *El tercermundismo* Rangel attempts to probe more deeply into the reasons why the Third World reacts negatively to free enterprise, development, and what he calls the "unescapable demand for modernization." Apparently, and here prodevelopmentalists as well as antidevelopmentalists might agree, there is something perverse in an attitude that rejects the material benefits that modernization and development bring. The explanation, Rangel feels, is obvious. The Third World—and Latin America is clearly included—simply does not respect the values and institutions of the developed world, chiefly, democracy and capitalism, which are inseparably linked in his view. He further suggests that the "dead weight" of customs and attitudes derived from indigenous societies accounts for these antimodern attitudes (*T*, 215). Moreover, Rangel faults the leading theoreticians of developmentalism (Swedish social scientist Gunnar Myrdal, for example) for refusing to see that deep-seated cultural differences among societies may make their cleverly devised theoretical models almost useless. Thus Rangel feels that these professional developmentalists of the United Nations and its agencies (many of whom he considers sympathetic toward socialism) have had a vested interest in promoting the idea that the Third World's difficulties in achieving modernization and higher standards of living are not due to profound cultural differences or to any intrinsic failings. Rather, Rangel states, the "professional" developmentalists suggest that their backwardness is due to the fact that they are victims of exploitation by the rich and powerful nations of the West. And so, these experts "flatter the 'new countries' and contribute to reinforcing their obsession that they have no responsibility for their backwardness and do not have to make any physical or intellectual effort to overcome their poverty except to plead, beg, or threaten that they be indemnified for the supposed damages done them by the West" (T, 226).

Rangel's position as outlined above is, to say the least, extreme. It accords the United Nations and the theoretical developmentalists such as Myrdal a role quite similar to that of nationalist/Marxist propagandists in the sense that they all encourage Third World nations to deny any responsibility for their own problems and to accept simplistic "dependency" thinking. Not that Rangel is opposed to development: quite the contrary, he strongly favors industrialization and technological progress but, it must be remembered, on a Western, specifically North American, pattern. Moreover, he consistently downplays the very real physical dangers of development (pollution, climatic change, etc.) as he does the political and economic threat to Latin America. Not surprisingly, the views expressed in *El tercermundismo*, like those found in his earlier essay, have not been popular with many Latin Americans. More important, whether one agrees with his politics or not, Rangel's essay leaves readers who seek a more human, more existential view of the consequences of development and technology to Spanish Americans during the period unsatisfied.

Although the effects—good and bad—of development could be found everywhere throughout the hemisphere, it was in the cities that they became most evident. While "urbanism" for developmental theoreticians was a positive term suggesting growth and the adoption of highly desirable "urban values" by an increasing percentage of the society, for the general population it often meant leaving a familiar rural setting to seek better opportunities in the burgeoning metropolis. For the thousands and even millions unsuccessful in this quest it could also mean a desperate existence in the wretched *barriadas, collampas, villas miserias,* and other slums that rapidly sprang up on the fringes of the great cities. Even middle-class urbanites became troubled by the sheer growth of metropolitan centers during the period; thus the traditional preference of cultivated Latins for the *urbis* was steadily being undermined by the impersonality, overdevelopment, pollution, and alienating atmosphere of such megacities as Lima, Caracas, Buenos Aires, and Mexico City.

A number of essayists bear witness to these concerns. In some cases entire books have focused on the theme of the city and in many other recent essays it figures prominently in connection with other issues. As early as 1962, Peruvian essayist Sebastián Salazar Bondy published his provocatively titled *Lima la horrible* (Lima the horrible); in Argentina several books centered on urban themes have appeared, including Sebreli's *Buenos Aires, vida cotidiana y alienación*, noted in the previous chapter, Rodolfo Kusch's *De la mala vida porteña* (On the evil life of Buenos Aires, 1966), and José Luis Romero's *Latinoamérica: las ciudades y las ideas* (Latin America: Cities and ideas, 1976). The Mexicans—Monsiváis, Fuentes, and Zaid among others—have been very sensitive to questions dealing with the modern city, though none has produced a volume focused primarily on the subject.

As its title suggests, the tone of Salazar Bondy's essay is decidedly gloomy. Much of *Lima la horrible* deals with the city's history and historiography; in fact, the very weight of Lima's past seems to press down upon its populace as much as do its humid, frequently leaden skies. While Salazar Bondy is very much aware of the city's poverty and its new immigrants (desperately poor, uneducated country folk), his emphasis goes far beyond a mere diatribe against the social and economic inequalities that typically accompany urban growth. Rather, he sees Lima as a focal point for the inauthentic values and social climbing that characterize the nation as a whole. His sharp vignettes of the physical changes that the city had recently undergone bear this out: "chaotic architecture where Tudor and neo-colonial are mixed with contemporary styles slavishly copied from North American magazines."[6] After describing the various districts of the city from the squalid *barriadas* of the very poor, through the intermediate neighborhoods of the middle classes, to the luxurious homes of the wealthy, he discusses the pervasive desire among all classes to move higher on the socioeconomic ladder. He concludes that the root of this quest for higher status lies in a basic insecurity or "instability" of the populace: "the more unstable is one's status, the more frequently one wishes to achieve stability. And by whatever means" (*LH*, 51). The system, Salazar continues, encourages ruthless individualism and, perhaps most of all, a desperate faith in a stroke of good luck, or *triunfo*. For this reason, he holds, *limeños* (and Peruvians in general) are gamblers and ingenuously believe the promise made by the rich and powerful: "thus, professional politicians do not offer the people collective liberation through socioeconomic restructuring but rather free housing, free land, and free food . . . The gates to riches are opened by the lottery, by betting on the horses, . . . by the ridiculous contests that award houses, cars, TVs, or cash for coupons" (*LH*, 53). The "well-greased machinery of fraud," Salazar believes, has kept the masses from supporting genuine revolutionary activity, since "for Lima's masses socialism constitutes a threat, even for the poorest person in his slum shack . . . which he hopes to own with a legal property title" (*LH*, 54).

Although the foregoing observations constitute one of the major focal points of Salazar's essay, he presents in addition a rich, detailed canvas of *limeño* life. His comment on the superficiality of religious observance in his fifth chapter, "The Devout and Voluptuous City," is penetrating, though quite within the tradition of earlier writers such as Riva Agüero, Basadre, or González Prada. Chapter 6 deals with women in the city's past and present. Its title, "From the Woman in Wraps to Miss Peru," gives a hint of the author's point; namely, that women since colonial days have been forced by circumstances to exercise power through a kind of sexual negotiation. Whether she was a seventeenth-century aristocrat tantalizing men by showing only a well-turned ankle or a bikini-clad contestant for the title of Miss Peru of 1962, she seeks the same objective: "a connection with a powerful man, and by means of him, a situation of power for herself" (*LH*, 78). The balance of *Lima la horrible* reinforces the general tone of the essay. Lima is presented as a rather ugly, poorly planned metropolis whose empty spaces are constantly assaulted by the sandy wasteland just beyond its limits. Salazar Bondy's romantic insistence upon the theme of an inhospitable nature ever encroaching upon the city is reminiscent of this motif in the work of the Argentines—Borges, whom he mentions in this connection (*LH*, 90), and Ezéquiel Martínez Estrada. Upon completing the essay one has the general feeling that Lima is a city on the defensive (Salazar reminds us it was originally designed as a military post) and that its inhabitants are constantly driven to seek refuge from their deep-seated insecurity. Social climbing provides one of these defensive measures, as does the evocation of the city's mythic past, what Salazar calls the "colonial utopia." An especially penetrating analysis of sociolinguistic features of Lima's culture demonstrates how satire, ambiguity, the calculated whisper, flattery, dissimulation, and the like serve as protective shields (*LH*, 94–97). Though this discussion is based solely on Peruvian material, readers familiar with texts such as Paz's *Laberinto de la soledad* or Cuban Jorge Mañach's early essay *Indagacíon del choteo* (Investigation of the *choteo*, 1928) will immediately see many fascinating parallels in this kind of sociolinguistic analysis. On balance, Salazar Bondy's elegantly written essay, while it does reflect the recent impact of development on urban life, belongs as much to the tradition of Paz, Martínez Estrada, and the other seekers of national identity as it does to the new *ensayismo* of 1960 to 1985.

We have already examined portions of *Buenos Aires, vida cotidiana y alienación* in connection with the discussion of revolution and rebellion. The main thrust of Sebreli's essay is, however, aimed at describing the dull, dehumanized life of lower- and middle-class *porteños* of the mid-1960s. Early on he attempts to put his text within the framework of a kind of humanized sociology in which the author, unlike writers of "the gray and monotonous world of sociological statistics," treats real people and is himself enmeshed in the material under examination. His mentors in this endeavor appear to be Jean-Paul Sartre (quoted in the book's epigraph), along with Americans Thorsten Veblen, C. Wright Mills, and Lewis Mumford (*BA*, 13). Whether Sebreli's style and originality bear comparison with this distinguished group of sociological essayists may be left to the reader's judgment; at any rate, his essay does offer an interesting view of Buenos Aires during the early decades of the post-Perón period.

Though a Marxist (and a very "pure" one, as we have already noted), Sebreli curiously pays relatively little attention to the really poor, the lumpen of the *villas miserias;* rather, he centers his examination on the middle class, a sector he apparently knows well and for whom he shows considerable disdain. He paints a particularly dismal picture of the lower middle class, those who live in rented tenement apartments, "narrow rooms, thin walls through which shouts, conversation and radio programs are filtered . . . long, dark, basementlike hallways with sooty air from kitchen smoke . . . windows with clothes hanging out . . . [in] gray paved courtyards" (*BA*, 68). The lifelong dream of those who live in these circumstances, he points out, is to own their own home: these aspirations, encouraged by the establishment, make these people, poor as they may be, staunch defenders of private property. It may be recalled that Salazar Bondy noted essentially the same phenomenon among the poor of Lima. Sebreli's view of the districts to which the lowest strata of the middle class aspire is almost as dreary as his description of the tenements. In these suburbs (some in the established neighborhoods, but many on the newly developed western fringe of the city) he finds depressing architectural monotony, bad taste, and, in contrast to older "unplanned" districts, boredom and desperation:

> frightful labyrinths of order and common sense, where it is as difficult to lose oneself as to find oneself. Despite the relatively citified, hygienic value they may have, these neighborhoods repel us because of their mediocrity, because of their lack of antagonism, of conflict, of drama, of adventure that constitutes the attraction of the older, unplanned districts of the city. The latter may, at times, lead to crime, but the former inevitably engender boredom, sadness, and anguish.
>
> The inhabitants of these look-alike houses, with their same little dwarf statues in their gardens, with the same fake period furniture, with the same magnificent kitchens, are very much alike, although

everyone thinks of themselves as superior to their neighbors; they have similar jobs, they vote more or less for the same parties, and they have identical, fixed, and immutable views of the world. (*BA*, 69)

A good deal of Sebreli's essay is devoted to this merciless dissection of the urban and suburban middle class. Again, like Salazar Bondy he notes this group's passion for social climbing and their ceaseless efforts to gain status by trying to appear richer and more important. Paralleling his Peruvian counterpart (as well as Paz of the *Laberinto*), Sebreli finds dissimulation, a "closed" attitude toward others, and the use of linguistic subterfuge as typical of the Buenos Aires bourgeoisie:

> the enormous difference between what the middle class wishes or imagines itself to be and what it actually is forces it to live in hiding and dissimulation, closing itself off from any frank and open communication and always maintaining a cold distance from others. In the pointless petulance of its ceremonious gestures, its precious language of circumlocutions, and its overly proper clothing, it reveals insecurity with regard to other classes and a sense of shame and humiliation because of its own insignificance.
>
> In a society that equates status with wealth, where property is the only means of gaining recognition, the middle class is condemned to use everything that it possesses to appear to have what it lacks, to deceive with cheap tinsel. (*BA*, 88–89)

In addition to their penchant for show and false posturing, the middle-class *porteño*, Sebreli notes, seeks escape from alienation and underlying insecurity by many other "unauthentic" means: TV with its soap operas, popular magazines, sports, excessive concern over food, and the cult of popular heroes (*BM*, 88). One such popular icon discussed in some detail is the celebrated tango singer of yesteryear, Carlos Gardel. A classic rags-to-riches type, his photo adorns bars, the dashboard of city buses, and the walls of the poorest homes. He is the archetypical self-made man, a winner in the game of life; most important, he operates strictly as an individual, a loner, because unborn group efforts and social action are meaningless. Thus Sebreli finds that in the myth of "Gardelism" and among those who identify with it "there is no content of social vindication . . . there is no attack against any existing structure . . . Gardel's world is fixed and immutable, with its rich and poor, its winners and losers . . . Gardel, an opportunist and adventurer, is only concerned about the stability of his own situation" (*BA*, 130). As elsewhere, Sebreli seems naively disappointed that the lower classes gravitate toward this kind of model rather than toward lines of political commitment. In a similar vein, he decries the factory worker who, after long hours of alienating toil, seeks diversion in the usual popular outlets such as the soccer stadium rather than visiting public libraries, attending lectures, or participating in the affairs of the union hall (*BA,* 176). In short, Sebreli finds Buenos Aires's lower classes pursuing superficial pleasures, many of which are products of new technology or of foreign pop culture: "they dance rock or the twist more than the tango and their only aspiration is for immediate pleasure" (*BA,* 186). At the essay's conclusion the theme of the modern city as an alienating force seems subsumed to the author's plea that the Argentine left, and its leaders, learn how to inspire those who now lead unauthentic, alienated lives to abandon the path of self-interest and immediate satisfaction. His final hope is that the masses will then be able to live "with generosity, with authenticity, with joy and lucidity." Precisely how, when, and under what conditions this utopian vision will be realized is never quite made clear.

A number of other Argentine essayists have taken similar positions regarding urban development and the alienating nature of life in the megalopolis. Ernesto Sábato, for example, treats these themes at some length in his collection *Apologías y rechazos* (Apologies and rejections, 1979). In a revealingly titled chapter, "A Model for Disaster," he warns his compatriots to consider carefully what the results of *technolatría* ("technolatry") have been in the advanced countries. In a tone reminiscent of Sebreli he describes the workers of any modern city: "on leaving their factories and offices in which they are slaves of computers and other machinery, they enter the domain of mass sports or the illusory world of cheap novels and TV series [also] produced by machines."[7] He repeatedly characterizes modern man as "stripped of individual attributes" or as an "object" not unlike a factory product; in short, as dehumanized. Elsewhere in his essay he calls for "authentic communities" and the "decentralization of cities" to counteract the pernicious effects of "growing centralization, mad technology . . . the Super-State, and . . . the reification of man" (*AR,* 135). Further examples of these concerns—that the competitive, self-interested life of the modern city might someday be replaced by a more humane communitarian urban society—are also evident in Rodolfo Kusch's rather poetic *De la mala vida porteña,* an essay that can only be noted here, in José Luis Romero's *Latinoamérica: las ciudades y las ideas,* and in several of Julio Mafud's essays, notably the previously discussed *El hombre nuevo.*

This view of Spanish America's cities as centers of alienation, inauthenticity, and false values is confirmed by writers throughout the continent. Uruguay's Eduardo Galeano, for example, is an eloquent witness to this situation in his previously cited *Las venas abiertas de América Latina* and in his more recent *Voces de nuestro tiempo* (Voices of our times, 1981). In his description of Caracas, written during his travels as a political exile, he paints a picture of a basically ugly city glutted with oil-produced wealth but one in which the bulk of the population continues to live in the same poverty that obtained back in the days when Venezuela was a poor agricultural country:

> Caracas . . . has grown sevenfold in thirty years; the patriarchal city of cool patios, broad plazas, and a silent cathedral has seen skyscrapers rise up at the same rate as oil derricks have sprouted on Lake Maracaibo. Today it is a supersonic, noisy, air-conditioned nightmare, a center of oil culture that could be the true capital of Texas. Caracas chews gum and loves synthetic products and canned foods; it wears disposable garments, it never walks, it moves only by automobile; it has trouble sleeping, because it cannot quench its desire to buy, to consume, . . . to spend, to use, to appropriate everything.[8]

Galeano presents an even more wretched view of the city when he describes its slums, where half a million people subsist as onlookers outside the economy of consumerism: "on the hills around Caracas half a million forgotten souls watch, from their huts built of refuse, the extravagance of others . . . in the culture of consumption, not everyone consumes. Every fifteen years the number of Venezuelan children who die of disease and malnutrition reaches a figure higher than that of the entire population of Maracaibo" (*VA*, 257). The desperation of the poor living on the city's outer perimeter of slums seems, in Galeano's passionate prose, to be intensified by the presence of the wealthy sector's high-tech society. The Charneca district had to be bulldozed because its squalor could be seen from some of the windows of the four-star Caracas Hilton; and ironically, in the worst slum shacks every Sunday afternoon desperate men gather round the radio or television (essentials even for those who cannot afford food or medicine) to get the latest results from the Rinconada track, where society gathers for the ritual of thoroughbred racing (*VA*, 112–113).

The culture of Spanish America's burgeoning cities is for Galeano essentially bad, not only because it perpetuates—if not exacerbates—the economic inequalities of the continent, but also because it exalts foreign, especially North American, values among all classes. While this pursuit of the alien "good life" may be simply ugly and tasteless among the wealthy, among the poor it leads to frustration and violent outlets: gambling, drug addiction, and general delinquency. Moreover, as others have also observed, it is the youth who fall prey most easily to the manipulators of consumerism. Thus Galeano, like Sebreli and others, finds the revolutionary potential of the urban poor, especially young people, undermined and subverted by big business operating through the media. A TV commercial for Celanese Corporation's new line of blue jeans illustrates this point well. " 'Rebel,' it [the ad] advises them . . . 'Buy your rebelliousness by buying *Lois* jeans' " (*VA*, 114).

Doubts concerning the ultimate benefits of progress, reactions to the unthinking pursuit of development, apprehension regarding the apparently "foreign" nature of emerging technological society, and the view of the city as the locus of alienating, uncontrolled growth all come together with extraordinary force in the work of the Mexican essayists. This group, whom we have already met in the preceding chapter, has been exceptionally well positioned to take up these questions. With the largest population of all Spanish-speaking countries, with its proximity to the exemplar of technological societies, the United States, and with the largest metropolis in the hemisphere, if not the world, Mexico by the 1960s found itself facing a host of urgent problems.[9] Like most Spanish American capitals, Mexico City has become the point at which the forces of development, technology, demographic shifts, and social change all converge. It is not surprising, then, that the city itself should occupy a central position in the writings of essayists such as Monsiváis, Fuentes, Zaid, and others. The first of these has a special relationship to his native city. Like his literary precursor of the 1920s, Salvador Novo, Monsiváis may be considered a "chronicler of the city"—a writer who often expresses his love/hate relationship to the metropolis in sharply drawn, intense vignettes and at other times in the broadest of satirical strokes. In his two collections of the period, *Días de guardar* and *Amor perdido*, he presents the full socioeconomic gamut of Mexico City life: he explores such things as the desperate mythology of the poorest slum dwellers, the pretensions of the middle class, and the conspicuous consumption of the new rich. Throughout, his dazzling prose style—which will be treated in greater detail in a later chapter—relies upon nonlinear presentation along with a marked penchant for caricature. Like his mentor, Novo, Monsiváis has a fine eye for significant detail. His sketches of the city's most representative and symbolically richest *barrios* illustrate this perfectly. Thus, of the new construction in the Tlatelolco district (the scene of the student massacre of 1968), he observes, "The buildings . . . extend an act of state will: one must think in terms of gigantic proportions that exercise our inferiority complex and prove us to be the equal of any nation. What does this architecture express? . . . It expresses the will of Mexico's leaders to escape the realities of the times" (*AP*, 43). Acutely sensitive to the city's history, Monsiváis notes the new urban geography created by the influx of the rural masses and its effect on other sectors of the population: "by the fifties the architectural chaos and the changes imposed by the migration and sexual incontinence of the masses make obligatory the disappearance of city pride, replaced by class vanity, multiplied by individual ambition for recognition" (*AP*, 292). This process, he notes, leads to "a series of unchecked impulses toward expansion and consumption," while the media increasingly hide and make invisible the "growing copper-skinned masses which so bother the elite" (*AP*, 292). The city's middle class, meanwhile, responds by insisting that Mexico City be transformed into a cosmopolis, the equal of and similar to all other great urban centers of Europe or North America. This desire to emulate "other mythologies and other geopolitical centers" has expressed itself in the flourishing Pink Zone (Zona Rosa) of the city, an area well known to tourists and natives alike for its boutiques, art galleries, fine restaurants, sophisticated habitués, and overall cosmopolitan atmosphere. Monsiváis's rich though idiosyncratic description merits extensive citation:

> Concentrated in the Federal District the Mexican bourgeoisie turns abroad in search of amulets against boredom and the sense of insignificance. It wishes to be judged not by its own intrinsic worth but rather by what it reveres, and as a result it has decided to share myths and fashions with the bourgeoisie of the developed world. The days of national distinctiveness have passed, and it becomes more convenient to accept the role of a progressive suburban colony which, around the early sixties, exploded into the fantasyland of the Zona Rosa, the final effort of a reverential geography tipped in favor of bourgeois demands. . . . Here one can be a millionaire or a great thinker while in New York or Paris one is an unknown nobody. The Zona Rosa is the final product of a series of colonial hallucinations: internal exile, the elite that gains luster by virtue of the surrounding barbarism, the elegance that is not recognized internationally . . . The Zone . . . is the free territory of universalism. To its orthodoxy belong the cine-clubs . . . karate classes, concerts of electronic music, the dress circle . . . For the Zone a monstrous paradox is no longer the begging child contemplating (with the obligatory nose pressed against the window) an endless Christmas dinner, but rather a '46 Chevy alongside a Porsche. Painters, writers, TV models, musicians, and filmmakers see in the legend of a gilded artist's life a strategy to halt the capital city's decline. (*AP*, 293)

A careful reading of this passage reveals that Monsiváis's description of the Pink Zone's glamor and glitz is permeated by a sense of impending doom and by a none-too-gentle unmasking of the pretensions of the newly rich. This interpretation is supported by Monsiváis's own unambiguous comments. He points out that Mexico City's mood of the 1960s—as epitomized by the Zona Rosa—was sharply changed by the events of Tlatelolco and by steadily growing problems of hyperdevelopment: "anarchy in prices, the housing crisis, the water shortage, unobtainable transportation, the traffic problem, eight thousand tons of garbage per day, the general stress of daily life, unhealthy conditions, insufficient sewage and public lighting, pollution, lack of medical services, . . . delinquency, overpopulation . . . with its burden of hovels and outer perimeter of slums" (*AP*, 294). But what seems to perturb Monsiváis as much, if not more, than these problems themselves are the attitudes that have helped to create them and the attitudes that they in turn perpetuate. The blind pursuit of development, aided and abetted by Mexico's government, is, in his view, a major culprit: "what exactly does *desarrollismo* propose? The unchallenged advantages of any kind of growth, the cult of growth for its own sake. Our governments, every six years, are founded upon this premise and they thus foment, considering it a triumph, the over-expansion of the city" (*AP*, 293). Perhaps worst of all is the end result of this process. The uncontrollable problems of rampant urbanism breed a kind of helpless acceptance of the situation—a "stupified consciousness," to use Monsiváis's exact terminology, in which "the mood of catastrophe takes charge" and the "ominous future hides the ominous present" (*AP*, 294).

This picture of the flamboyant Zona Rosa is only one example of Monsiváis's exploration of Mexico City's urban geography. His poetic canvas of the Colonia Roma district in *Días de guardar* illustrates his fondness for historical evocation. Roma, now a somewhat down-at-the-heels neighborhood, was toward the turn of the century and in succeeding decades the bastion of the middle-class bureaucrat—the plodding governmental *funcionario* whose modest personal ambitions reflected his "petrified" life-style. Monsiváis appears to be saying that the district, with its typical belle époque facades, gabled roofs, and ornate metalwork, has lost its original raison d'être, that its physical appearance no longer has the semiotic force of yesteryear. In sum, the district has become one of the many "phantasmagoric communities, transmuted into relics of urban development, that today are only frequented by collectors of existential museums. These internal 'ghost towns' are irrefutable evidence . . . [of] the death of a certain form of urban existence" (*DG*, 278). The underlying motif that informs Monsiváis's vignette of Colonia Roma is that the district represents the lost illusions of a class whose pretensions and dreams of continued upward mobility were shattered by the new society emerging with the revolution of 1910.

Some of Monsiváis's richest pages, and ones that bear directly on questions of development, are those describing Mexico City's worst slums. In addition to essays focused on such districts as Tepito or Candelaria, the presence of the nation's poor and the culture of poverty surface in many texts that deal with other subjects. Occasionally a seemingly offhand remark in these pieces can be very significant. For example, in his lively essay on José Alfredo Jiménez, one of the nation's most celebrated singers of *música ranchera* (a genre somewhat similar to North American country and western), the psychology of the "loser"—the traditionally downtrodden *desgraciado* that haunts the lyrics of this music—is viewed in the context of urban growth, high tech, and big business. Jiménez, he notes, "is, among other things, the first to bear witness to [the coming] of the rural immigrants, the recent settlers in the city of Mexico: as such he will begin as the bearer (urban life with an agrarian memory) of the vicissitudes and loss of traditions that poverty . . . produces" (*AP*, 89). Monsiváis's detailed analysis of the precise relationship between the purveyors of pop culture—in this case, *ranchera* singers, record companies, the film industry, and so on—cannot be traced here. Very briefly, and perhaps over-simplified, he sees the impoverished, unsophisticated, and exploited country people crowded into urban slums where, lacking any genuine means of expressing their many frustrations, they identify with the world of *música ranchera*, a world, Monsiváis suggests, of simple prefabricated emotions, of synthetic rural memories created by commercially motivated manipulators whose stylized product, rather than reflecting an authentic reality, is shaped to conform to "the ideas that the masses have of their likes and antecedents" (*AP*, 94).

Monsiváis's long essay "Tepito as a Legend" in *Días de guardar* represents his most penetrating view of the urban poor, their psychology, and their heroes. To be born in slums like Tepito or Candelaria, he affirms, "is to subject oneself to the ecology of 'a lost city.' " He further states that these crime-ridden districts of "dilapidated *pulquerías* (low taverns where *pulque*, a cheap fermented liquor is sold), drugs, vice, robbery, of no quarter asked and none given" stand for "the final resistance to order" (*DG*, 279) as epitomized in the cult of petty criminals, sports heroes, and especially prizefighters. The basic psychology of the slum, he notes, is expressed by a kind of skeptical doubt "in the face of the dogma of triumph." Monsiváis finds the perfect symbol of this attitude in the figure of the boxer "El Chango" Casanova: "the 'born loser' . . . the collector of disaster, the typical Mexican, buddy" (*DG*, 280). Thus, the slum dweller identifies with archetypes of fatalistic acceptance; he shrugs his shoulders and takes life as it comes. After all, he cynically remarks, "nobody ordered you to be born here" (*DG*, 285). Monsiváis concludes his essay on a rather poetic note: "no one can escape destiny, the classical chorus had said; you should have told me you were from the Third World, one would say today. The country as a prison, the city as a prison, the *barrio* as a prison, the prison as a prison" (*DG*, 285).

While Monsiváis and some of the other Mexicans treat problems of the city and the underlying issue of development at considerable length, it is Gabriel Zaid who approaches them with the freshest viewpoint and sharpest eye. A native of the bustling industrial city of Monterrey, Zaid combines the rare gifts of a poet with the hard-nosed pragmatism of an industrial engineer who has spent a good deal of his life only a few miles from the U.S. border. By comparison with his fellow essayists of more traditional origins and background, Zaid's thinking is iconoclastic, independent, and, like his birthplace, eccentric in the literal sense. His writing career began in the mid-sixties with several contributions to major journals such as the *Revista de la Universidad de México*, two books on poetic interpretation, *La máquina de cantar* (The singing machine, 1967) and *Leer poesía* (Reading poetry), followed by collaboration on important periodicals such as *Diálogos*, *La Cultura en México*, *Plural*, and *Vuelta*. As noted earlier, the charmingly titled *Cómo leer en bicicleta* and perhaps his most serious work, *El progreso improductivo*, appeared in the late seventies.

As these titles suggest, Zaid's interests are extremely broad: poetics, economics, politics, and Mexican culture are all major concerns. But it is when he brings his unique viewpoint and wry humor to bear upon such things as popular beliefs, contemporary fads, middle-class pretensions, and especially the unthinking worship of *desarrollismo* that his work is most impressive. At first glance his *El progreso improductivo* appears to be a rather technical treatise: its pages contain statistical tables, considerable economic terminology, and chapter headings that might deter all but the most devoted students of the Dismal Science. However, on closer inspection it becomes clear that we are not dealing with a typical social scientist but rather with a spirit more akin to a Jonathan Swift or (if a contemporary comparison is needed) a George Will. Like that of his eighteenth-century soulmate, Zaid's writing is rich in "modest proposals." At one point he asks, Why not help the economy by taxing the traditional Mexican *mordida* (a bribe paid to a person in authority)?[10] In another context he wonders if the logical conclusion of much meliorist thinking should not be the elimination of all those who do not have a real chance to be wealthy: "castrate anyone who cannot demonstrate that he is a millionaire" (*PI*, 76). In his sly piece on "Children as a Business" he writes of children as "the product" and even suggests a cost analysis of reproduction among the rural poor compared with the university-educated class:

> Let us review the great cost differences that exist in the economic
> management of two not very well defined prototypes: the peasant and
> the university graduate.
>
> a) The time of coitus, in both cases, involves no costs, because it is
> done (normally) on working days and is usually considered (under
> normal conditions) to be a satisfaction.
>
> But in the case of the university person, in addition to time, there
> are other cost factors. Industrial expenses, such as books on love without fear, contraceptives, deodorants, perfumes, lingerie, etc. Professional services, such as psychoanalysis, orientation meetings, courses in
> interpersonal relations, and even practice sessions, directed by doctors
> and nurses, on having better orgasms. (*PI*, 32)

Despite this tongue-in-cheek authorial voice, or perhaps by virtue of it, Zaid is a serious critic of his times and of his country. Though the underlying critical ideas in *El progreso improductivo* are not in themselves very unusual, in the context of contemporary Mexico bent on growth, industrialization, and modernity they certainly provide a refreshing counterbalance to those who pursue progress for progress' sake, to developmentalists who fail to recognize the nature of the Third World's basic needs, and to planners who forever design increasingly complex projects. His thinking is all the more impressive since the alternatives he proposes are not typical ones. Neither a Marxist, nor a reactionary, nor a flower-child, Zaid combines ideas from many sources. Eclectic and pragmatic, he shuns ideology for its own sake; he espouses ideas that work, that offer a reasonable hope for social or economic improvement. Thus, at times he echoes the "small is beautiful" minimal technology of a Schumacher (*PI*, 133–134); on another occasion he suggests that instead of providing "make work" for the poor that cash be distributed among the lowest economic strata—a kind of "negative income tax" plan (*PI*, 92–93).

Much of Zaid's attention is directed toward the problems created by the influx of poor, uneducated *campesinos* into the city. Here again his thinking is quite unorthodox: in the first place he is very much aware of the fact that modern urban bourgeoisie—especially Latins—have a deep-seated disdain for rural life, though they may of course enjoy a weekend in the country or owning a rustic vacation home. He takes special joy in pointing out that his leftist friends also share this disdain and that Marx himself wrote of "the idiocy of country life" in contrast to the vibrant, creative life of the city. What he finds most disturbing are the efforts made to convert every *campesino* into a modern consumer of automobiles, a university education, urban housing, and so on. As a result, the cities have become overcrowded, and the insufficient supply of jobs, housing, and educational services produces severe social problems, frustrations, ecological damage, and the growth of slums. He points out that by making country life attractive in the first place, the absurd cycle of country-to-city-back-to-country, a process that might take many generations, could be obviated: "a curious cycle of aspirations: leave the country, go to the city, have a university career, own a car and become prosperous to the point of getting a house in the country . . . Is this the long round-trip journey that we propose for the *campesinos* in two, three, or a thousand generations? Would it not be more practical and even less costly to immediately expedite a fully human life in the country?" (*PI*, 61) Zaid is somewhat vague in explaining what should be done to achieve this goal. However, his fondness for Vasco de Quiroga's sixteenth-century vision of a utopian society in rural Mexico perhaps hints at the nature of this ideal social order (*PI*, 64), as do his frequent references to "appropriate technology" for the rural masses. In this regard he suggests that the poor would do well to rely upon breast-feeding infants rather than buy expensive powdered milk formulas, or that using the efficient domestic *molino de nixtamal* for grinding flour makes more sense than selling grain and then buying commercially prepared flour (*PI*, 150–151). The notion that a relatively poor country can be modern to only a limited degree and still be happy runs through much of Zaid's thinking. Similarly, he apparently holds to the idea that not everyone can or should attempt to rise to the apex of the socioeconomic pyramid. Yet this seemingly elitist view is balanced by faith in individual effort and talent to overcome the "disadvantage" of living in less than modern circumstances. After all, he observes, "practically all the dignity, culture, and elegance that humanity has produced for millennia has been the work of people without automobiles or university degrees" (*PI*, 61). Finally, it would be difficult to find two writers more dissimilar in authorial tone and political outlook than Gabriel Zaid and Julio Cortázar, whose sly comment on progress set the stage for this chapter. Yet a comparison of the Mexican's essay with Cortázar's text reveals that the underlying thinking of both derive from very similar doubts regarding progress and technology.

Further evidence that these attitudes are held by a wide range of authors may be found in the work of a writer not usually thought of as an essayist, yet Carlos Fuentes, a leading figure in the 1960s "boom" in Spanish American fiction, has produced a substantial corpus of articles and commentaries that clearly merit consideration as examples of the genre. A number of these pieces have been collected in three widely circulated volumes: a literary study, *La nueva novela latinoamericana* (The new Latin American novel, 1967), and two books dealing with social and political problems, *Casa de dos puertas* (A house with two doors, 1970) and the previously noted *Tiempo mexicano*. It is the last of these that bears most directly on the themes we have been pursuing.

Fuentes argues that the dramatic events of 1968, specifically the Tlatelolco massacre, indicated a general political bankruptcy of the Mexican system. He also points out that this collapse was inextricably linked with severe economic disjuncture in the country. He finds that inequitable distribution of land, demographic shifts, and especially the infatuation with *desarrollismo* lie at the root of the problem (*TM*, 173ff.). True to the spirit of the literary essay, Fuentes avoids abstract economic discussion and seeks explanations in broadly human terms. Thus, his brilliant piece on "Nuestra señora la Pepsicoátl" (Our lady of Pepsicoátl), which appears early in *Tiempo mexicano*, delves deeply into such matters as Mexican myth and national character along with the specious enticements of rapid economic development. He points out that "many urban sectors of Mexico . . . have succeeded in realizing the dream of modern progress and have been able—almost—to live in Monterrey as if in Milan . . . or in Mexico City as if in Los Angeles. This goal, however, has been achieved, again, at an inopportune moment: it has coincided with uprisings, the destruction of the environment, pollution, urban ghettos" (*TM*, 32–33). In short, Fuentes wonders if Mexico's infatuation with *desarrollismo* has been worth the trouble, if perhaps it would not be better to devise a more appropriate national model of development. Yet, he argues, there can be no "return to Quetzalcoátl" or any facile cultivation of a hybrid society, the "Pepsicoátl" image in which plasticized North American culture is superimposed upon an equally false romanticized nativism: "Quetzalcoátl promised us the Sun; Pepsicoátl promises us a Bendix washing machine on an easy payment plan." But the fruits of Pepsicoátl worship are indeed bitter: in the long run they are synonymous with urban blight, poverty, and injustice. In a final well-wrought image Fuentes observes that "the children of Zapata . . . will become the children of Sánchez" (*TM*, 34).

Whether they are Argentines such as Sebreli or Mafud writing about the alienating culture of modern Buenos Aires, a Peruvian such as Salazar Bondy contemplating Lima as an ugly showcase for false values, an exile like Galeano describing the Caracas of the seventies as a Texaslike air-conditioned nightmare, or Monsiváis, Zaid, and Fuentes analyzing their nation's devotion to Pepsicoátl, Mexico's plasticized god of development, all these essayists are sharply critical of Spanish America's—and by extension the Third World's—headlong rush to replicate the technological paradise of the developed nations, especially the United States. Not that they wish to preserve agrarian or indigenous utopias that never really existed. Rather, as genuine dissenters from popular trends and from the grandiose plans of the establishment, they suggest that notions of progress and development must not be accepted unconditionally but on terms more human in scope and more appropriate to the region.

As has so often been the case regarding the major concerns of Hispanic America, and indeed the entire world, it is Octavio Paz who offers the most eloquent and most unanswerable meditations on these matters. In his very provocative essay of 1970, *Posdata*, his critique of development is unequivocal: "this model [of development] does not correspond to our true historic, psychic, and cultural reality but it is rather a mere copy (and a degraded copy) of the North American archetype . . . Development has been, until now, the opposite of what the word signifies: to spread out that which is wound up, to unfold, to grow freely and harmoniously. Development has been a veritable straitjacket. A false liberation: although it has done away with many ancient and senseless prohibitions it has also burdened us with demands that are no less horrible and onerous."[11] And earlier in the same text his comment on the related theme of progress is equally impressive. "The philosophy of progress at last shows us its true face: a blank, featureless face. We now know that the kingdom of progress is not of this world: the paradise that it promises us is in the future, an untouchable, unreachable, perpetual future. Progress has populated history with technological marvels and monsters but has made a desert of human life. It has given us more things, not more being" (*P*, 76). This questioning of progress and of what may be considered the ideology of development is, however, only a partial aspect of a more general reappraisal of ideology in broadest terms, the subject of the chapter that follows.

The Twilight of Ideology

FOUR

Some thirty years ago American sociologist Daniel Bell published a widely discussed study, *The End of Ideology*. Though he was not a Latin Americanist or a student of literature, what he wrote at that time bears noting in the context of recent trends in the Spanish American essay. In very general terms what Bell described over three decades ago was a historical process among Western intellectuals—society's "floating stratum," to cite an earlier writer, Karl Mannheim—of "objectively and disinterestedly" adopting a total ideology which becomes "an all-inclusive system of comprehensive reality . . . a set of beliefs, infused with passion [that] seeks to transform the whole of a way of life."[1] This "secularized religion," he notes, can take many forms: in common usage we often speak of less totalized world-views as the "ideology" of the businessman, of the liberal, or, on a more abstract level, of the American egalitarian "dream." However, early in his argument he makes the important point that since the nineteenth century the term "ideology" has become "a product of the left and [has] gained a distinctive resonance in that context" (*EI*, 19).[2] The core of Bell's argument is that by 1960 intellectuals throughout the West were abandoning all ideologies, but especially the "secular religion" sponsored by Marxism: "today, these ideologies are exhausted. The events behind this important sociological change are complex and varied. Such calamities as the Moscow trials, the Nazi-Soviet pact, the concentration camps, the suppression of the Hungarian workers form one chain; such social changes as the modification of capitalism, the rise of the Welfare State [form] another . . . This is not to say that such ideologies as communism in France and Italy do not have a political weight or a driving momentum from other sources.

But out of all this history one simple fact emerges: for the radical intelligentsia, the old ideologies have lost their 'truth' and their power to persuade" (*EI*, 402).

As I noted earlier Bell is not a Latin Americanist; however, the few references to the region in his 1960 work are germane to my concerns in the present chapter. Toward the close of the book's epilogue he characterizes the then emerging New Left as having passion and energy, little historical memory, and only hazy ideas of the future (*EI*, 405)—a description quite reminiscent of Paz's discussion of rebels as opposed to revolutionaries noted in the previous chapter. Bell goes on to state that the problems facing the New Left at the time were difficult ones; for example, workers' control as part of the "democratic planning" process and how to guard against the dangers of bureaucratization. He further observes that the New Left's typical answers to these and other tough questions were essentially fuzzy and rhetorical—"bravura phrases," to use his term. He then prophetically states that "it is in the attitudes toward Cuba and the new states in Africa that the meaning of intellectual maturity, and of the end of ideology, will be tested" (*EI*, 405). Bell concludes by voicing his fears that the New Left may not pass this test, that basic freedoms will be degraded, that means will justify ends, and that the demise of ideology will not lead to the end of vacuous rhetoric (*EI*, 406).

In the pages that follow I shall attempt, in a very general way, to extend Bell's line of thought to what can only be perceived as a gradual abandoning of ideology among Spanish American intellectuals, specifically the essayists. The starting point for this discussion must focus on the Cuban revolution and the ideological aura of the Castro regime. Of course, writings that may properly be called ideological essays were produced in Spanish America well before Fidel's march into Havana. The left, for example, was well represented in the work of Peru's nineteenth-century *pensador* Manuel González Prada or a few decades later by J. C. Mariátegui; and if we accept positivism or traditional nationalism as genuine ideologies (though I am not sure we should), then any number of nineteenth- and early twentieth-century writers might fall into this category. However, the Cuban phenomenon was—or, better stated, became—unique in that it attracted, focused, and nurtured a rich blend of heterodox Marxism, long-standing anti-Yankeeism, and a profound Hispanic cultural defensiveness that has been evident among many Latin American intellectuals, albeit in a rather ill-defined state, since the turn of the century. I suspect that no political movement or historical event of the present century has had a comparable impact upon the hemisphere's thinkers and writers.

The Cuban ideological aura, as I have termed it, was, however, almost nonexistent during the first few years of Castro's regime. As one student of the

Cuban revolution notes, "There are several factors that made it a difficult task to assess the nature and role of ideology in the Cuban revolution. Castro is not an ideologist and has shown little concern for ideology. Before its triumph the July 26 movement produced neither a coherent program nor an ideological scheme . . . If we exclude the early efforts made by Ernesto (Che) Guevara, it was only at the end of 1966, more than seven years after being in power, that the revolutionaries produced a formulation of hemispheric ideology."[3] The same observer, Carmelo Mesa-Lago, finds that a genuine Marxist ideological approach only became evident in Castro's speeches of the late 1960s, in some of Guevara's late writings, in the essays of the French supporter of Cuba, Regis Debray, and in various resolutions adopted by the Cubans in 1967. It is significant that Spanish America's writers lent their near unanimous, unconditional support to the regime precisely during this "pre-ideological" period. These were the years when the leading novelists—and essayists—of the "boom," Fuentes, Vargas Llosa, and others, enthusiastically hailed the revolution and in turn were published, discussed, and praised in Cuba's new literary journals. Fuentes, almost at the moment of Castro's triumph, was one of the first non-Cubans to laud the revolution: his position was seconded by the cream of Mexico's intelligentsia, including the dean of Spanish American essayists, Alfonso Reyes, who would die that same year.[4] And Chile's leading prose writer, José Donoso, in his revealing anecdotal essay *Historia personal del boom*, describes his reaction to the new Cuba of the early 1960s. He notes that despite the fact that he was essentially apolitical, he could not resist "the powerful wave of sympathy for a political cause that unified the continent and all its writers" and that gave "for a time a feeling of continental coherency."[5] Indeed, during the first two or three years of the regime, it would be difficult to find among the hemisphere's major writers a dissenting voice in this chorus of Cuban support.

However, by the late 1960s and culminating in 1971 (the year of the celebrated Padilla affair), a number of Cuba's literary supporters defected. Very likely it was not only the regime's drift toward Marxist ideology per se that led to this disaffection. One senses that it was a kind of disappointment that the appealing, youthful, freewheeling spirit of early *castrismo* was inevitably moving toward authoritarianism, bureaucratic repression, and a type of grimness that had become typical of everyday life in the Eastern bloc. The press of political and economic forces was, again, changing the joyful face of yet another *niña bonita*, to borrow a phrase from a different country and a different time.[6] Of course, some of our essayists—Fuentes, Paz, Vargas Llosa, or Chile's Jorge Edwards—very probably had strong reservations regarding ideology even before this period.

THE FAITHFUL

But before examining the reaction of these writers, some attention must be paid to those essayists whose work most clearly illustrates what may be considered orthodox leftist thinking. Among this group several figures come to mind: Argentine-born militant Ernesto "Che" Guevara (1928–1967), Uruguayan scholar Mario Benedetti (1920–), and Cuba's own Roberto Fernández Retamar (1930–), critic, poet, and director of the regime's foremost literary journal, *Casa de las Américas.*

The *Obra revolucionaria* (Revolutionary works, 1967) of the charismatic Che Guevara fills a substantial volume of over a thousand pages, and these writings represent only a partial selection of his speeches, articles, and memoirs. Yet one is hesitant to consider him a true essayist since the term suggests a degree of aesthetic consciousness, some sense of reshaping raw material, literary distancing—elements that are usually lacking in his prose. He perhaps comes closest to genuine literary creativity in some of the very personal anecdotal vignettes in his recounting of the military phase of the revolution, *Paisajes de la guerra revolucionaria* (Scenes of the revolution, 1963). More often than not his prose—straightforward and strong as it may be—is essentially technical in the sense that it serves a basically nonliterary purpose; as, for example, his well-known treatise *La guerra de las guerrillas* (*Guerrilla Warfare*, 1960). Despite these reservations regarding his status as an essayist, Guevara's political writings must be noted in any consideration of Cuban ideology. In his "Socialismo y el hombre en Cuba" (Socialism and man in Cuba, 1965), a good example of his work in this area, Guevara takes as his point of departure the frequently heard charge that communist society, especially in its early stages of construction, is characterized by "the abolition of the individual on the altar of the state."[7] Although he proposes to counter this classic criticism with specifics, he bases his refutation upon a familiar ideological position that harks back to a formulation of the people/leader relationship often associated with the German romantic thinkers Fichte and Herder. Thus he writes of the Cuban masses: "it is true that they unhesitatingly follow their leaders, above all Fidel Castro, but to the degree that he has gained the confidence that responds precisely to the full interpretation of the people's desires, to their aspirations" (*OR*, 628). In short, by some unexplained, mystical process the Leader intuits the needs and aspirations of the *Volk* and hence his directives cannot possibly run counter to individual desires. Though it is not stated in his text, Guevara obviously holds that all this operates without recourse to such bourgeois mechanisms as elected parliamentary bodies and the like. A number of other basic tenets of his ideology figure prominently in "El socialismo y el hombre en

Cuba": chief among these is his repeatedly stated belief that people will indeed work for "moral" (i.e., nonmaterial) incentives, that participation in the revolution develops this attitude, and that revolutionary education must instill this spirit in the young, especially those who did not have the experience of revolutionary activity during the early period of militancy (*OR*, 631). Pervading his text is a utopian vision of a future society in which work will be done freely and enthusiastically, "based on the Marxist understanding that man only achieves his full human condition when he produces without the goad of physical necessity to sell himself as merchandise" (*OR*, 633). Toward the conclusion of the essay he calls for the emergence of the *hombre nuevo* who will transcend not only the ideas of the past but also those of "our decadent and diseased century" (*OR*, 636). Finally, striking a chord that would later resound strongly in the writings of Benedetti and Retamar, Guevara observes that in the present time of struggle not all elements in the society have made the full transition toward revolutionary ideology and that those especially at fault are the intellectuals: "to sum up, the guilt of many of our artists and intellectuals lies in their original sin; they are not authentically revolutionary" (*OR*, 636).

Mario Benedetti is a prolific literary critic who has published much in his native Uruguay as well as in Cuba, a nation with whose cultural life he has become closely associated. While his interests center on literature, he has frequently become involved in the heated polemics concerning the relationships between intellectuals and politics. His views, as seen in several essays of the late 1960s and early 1970s, are typical of pro-Cuban orthodoxy. Thus, writing on "Las prioridades del escritor" (The writer's priorities), he rejects Vargas Llosa's position that writers—especially novelists—are by definition critics of the society in which they live. Benedetti holds that this may be so in bourgeois regimes, but that obviously in a socialist society, "their subversive character has been refuted."[8] He notes in the same text that the worldwide "literary clan" always closes ranks to protect writers against any charges of wrongdoing. He further attacks intellectuals for preferring "unsuccessful revolutions" which by their nature do not disturb the status quo over those movements (such as the Cuban revolution) that do in fact bring about radical change.[9] Not surprisingly, the article in question was published in the fall of 1971, in the midst of the controversy following the Padilla affair. Even before this crucial event Benedetti had emphasized the need for strong political commitment on the part of writers. For example, in his 1967 piece "Situación del escritor en América Latina" (The situation of the writer in Latin America) he takes as his point of departure the highly admired but essentially apolitical (some would say reactionary) writings of Jorge Luis Borges. While Benedetti cannot declare the Argentine author's work invalid because of his ideological deficiencies, he refuses to admit that Borges's literary achievements excuse him for his "infamous" political stance. He then places the entire question in the context of European attitudes versus the New World situation: unlike Europe, which has embraced Borges, Latin America has not yet "achieved the cool capacity to contemplate the world with a kind of intelligent boredom." In ringing prose Benedetti then proclaims that

> while Latin America continues being a volcano, while half of its inhabitants are illiterate, while hunger constitutes the most effective instrument of the dominant class's blackmail, while the U.S. considers that it has the right to pressure, to prohibit, to invade, to blockade, to assassinate, in short to keep us from exercising our full right to exist, and including our right to die on our own terms and without its costly technical assistance; while Latin America searches, albeit chaotically and clumsily, for its own destiny and minimum happiness, let us keep on thinking of writers as those who face a dual responsibility: that of their art and that of the real world.[10]

There can be no doubt that the Cuban revolution made a profound effect on Roberto Fernández Retamar's career as a writer. In the opening pages of his *Ensayo de otro mundo* (Essays of another world, 1967) he confesses that his earlier work, a book on contemporary Cuban poetry and a study of stylistics (both completed before the revolution), now "appeared to be centuries away."[11] His writing since the Castro victory has been characterized by a rich blend of scholarly perception, poetic insight, the "burning immediacy" of a journalist,[12] and, not infrequently, the political rhetoric of a true believer—a man ardently devoted to a cause. Retamar's comments on Spanish American culture often stimulate and provoke his readers; but unless one is a totally unquestioning supporter of the Castro regime and its ideology, his Manichaean division of the hemisphere's writers into the chosen and the damned can prove quite irritating. Stated simply, political or ideological considerations regularly take precedence over aesthetic analysis. In his better-known books such as the *Ensayo de otro mundo*, in his best-known essay *Calibán* (1971), and in the collection *Para el perfil definitivo del hombre* (Toward a definitive profile of man, 1981) this tendency is obvious. A typical example can be found in his defense of what he calls "functional instrumentality" as the "dominant" and, by implication, the most praiseworthy mode of Spanish American literature. This terminology is, unless I am greatly mistaken, synonymous with such notions as commitment, literature in service of a cause, old-fashioned social protest, and so on. At any rate, he takes issue with Alfonso Reyes, who held that writing in which this mode dominated produced "hybrid" texts and "ancillary" genres. The point is an interesting one, since it bears on the question of generic boundaries and definition. However, Retamar's main concern does not lie in the area of formal genre theory; rather, he strives to privilege those writers who have directly or indirectly championed the cause of the poor, the exploited, and the alienated. Thus he cites among the writings of the "dominant" mode the early seventeenth-century commentaries of El Inca Garcilaso de la Vega, the essays of Peruvian radical J. C. Mariátegui, the poetry of Pablo Neruda and César Vallejo, and certain speeches of Simón Bolívar and, significantly, Fidel Castro.[13] A more narrowly focused example of the same tendency may be seen when he discussed Carlos Fuentes, a writer whom he loathes. At the root of Retamar's attitude is the fact that while Fuentes has on occasion expressed a vague sympathy toward an amorphous, idealized Marxism, the Mexican novelist is, in his view, nothing more than a shrewd apologist for the right. Although Retamar grudgingly admits that *La muerte de Artemio Cruz* is a good novel, he chooses to draw attention to the book's anti-ideological—specifically anti-Marxist—passages. He is especially irked by the scene in which a man in his late twenties admits that at the university he was terribly taken with Marxism (even to the point of writing a thesis on the concept of surplus value), but that once having experienced the real world, he considers Marxism to be nothing more than a youthful stage through which one passes.[14] The foregoing appears toward the end of *Calibán*, a short text that provides an excellent compendium of Retamar's thinking.

Calibán was first published in the fall of 1971 in Cuba's government-supported literary journal, *Casa de las Américas*. Its appearance in the wake of the Padilla affair certainly is significant, yet despite some references to that event at the outset and a few later on, the main body of the essay consists, as its subtitle suggests, of "Notes toward a Discussion of Culture in Our America." *Calibán* takes as its point of departure the notion that culturally mestizo Latin America has traditionally been ignored, misunderstood, and denigrated by "Euro-North Americans" as "an apprenticeship, a rough draft or copy of European bourgeois culture" (*C*, 5). Unfortunately, Spanish Americans have often reinforced this view, the most notable example being that of Rodó, whose symbology, as set forth in his classic of 1900, *Ariel*, is roundly refuted by the Cuban essayist. As Retamar puts it, "Our symbol then is not Ariel, as Rodó thought, but rather Caliban. This is something that we, the mestizo inhabitants of these same isles where Caliban lived, see with particular clarity: Prospero invaded the islands, killed our ancestors, enslaved Caliban" (*C*, 14). He goes on to explain, "There is no real Ariel-Caliban polarity. both are slaves in the hands of Prospero, the foreign magician. But Caliban is the rude and unconquerable master of the island, while Ariel, a creature of the air, . . . is the intellectual" (*C*, 16). The foregoing gives only a rough idea of Retamar's erudite and often polemical essay. His etymological and literary pursuit of Caliban through texts ranging from Shakespeare and Montaigne to Renan and contemporary Third World writers provides much material for scholars to ponder.

The greater part of the essay, however, is far from a dispassionate discussion of literary symbols. Rather, Retamar expands upon his notions of Prospero as "slave master" or exploiter and of Ariel as the intellectual duped by the "foreign magician." When he attacks "Prospero" (read Cuba's enemies, especially the United States) he does so almost casually though with considerable vehemence. Thus, early in the essay—in a statement that demands some difficult historical transpositions—he suggests that North American racism offered "a coherent model that *its Nazi disciples* attempted to apply even to other European conglomerates" (*C*, 4, my emphasis). At another point in the essay he takes up the term "free world" as used by the Western bloc. His position in this regard is perfectly clear: freedom in a non-Marxist context is meaningless, and the "free world" is "the hilarious name that capitalist countries today apply to themselves and bestow in passing on their oppressed colonies and neo-colonies" (*C*, 36). In sum, Retamar feels little need to become involved in any detailed analysis of the society, politics, or values of his enemies; he obviously feels he needs only employ such tried-and-true rhetorical touchstones as "Yankee imperialism," "neocolonialism," or "capitalist exploitation" to convince his readers. One suspects that his message might be more persuasive had he in fact addressed these issues more seriously and in greater detail.

By contrast, his attack upon "Ariel"—the hemisphere's misguided if not corrupted intelligentsia, in terms of his revisionist view of Rodó's symbology— is more specific and more substantive. We have already noted his dislike of Carlos Fuentes; however, this is only the tip of the iceberg. Fuentes, he claims, represents the "so-called Mexican mafia," a group which, he maintains, supported the Cuban revolution at the outset but drew away as soon as it realized that the movement was in fact "Marxist-Leninist . . . a revolution that has in its forefront a worker-peasant alliance." He then goes on to point out how recently this same group, "taking advantage of the wild vociferation occasioned by a Cuban writer's month in jail, . . . broke obstreperously with Cuba" (*C*, 36). The unnamed "Cuban writer" was, of course, Heberto Padilla, now reduced to the status of a nameless nonperson. It may be noted parenthetically that Retamar's implication is that the protest against his government's handling of the Padilla affair was a trivial event used only as a pretext by a small group of Mexicans and their friends to denigrate the Castro regime. In fact, however,

the Cubans' gross suppression of literary freedom produced a worldwide reaction among Europeans as well as Spanish Americans of many countries.[15] In
broader perspective Fuentes and his ilk are merely the contemporary expression of what Retamar calls a "now-powerless class"; namely, the European-
oriented bourgeoisie of the New World who, among other sins, have embraced
the ideas of Argentina's celebrated essayist of the past century, Domingo Faus-
tino Sarmiento. I shall not attempt to sketch out in any detail Retamar's critique of the latter's basic construct, "civilization" versus "barbarism," except
to say that like other anti-Sarmiento revisionists he employs selective citation
and sweeping generalizations to paint the nineteenth-century essayist as an
exploiter of the popular classes, an apologist for slavery, and a confirmed racist
who would "transport bourgeois policies of the metropolitan centers (particularly those of North America) to his own country" (*C*, 27). There is some truth
in this view, but it is also unilateral and ahistoric, and—for anyone seriously
interested in the subject—it ignores the important difference in Sarmiento's
thought of 1845, as expressed in *Facundo* and the more vulnerable positions
found in his *Conflicto y armonías de las razas en America* of 1883. At any rate,
Retamar hastens to point out that the "grotesque" ideas of Sarmiento have
found their modern avatar in the person of Jorge Luis Borges.

The discussion of the Argentine master in *Calibán* is an interesting mélange
of Retamar's parsimonious admiration and convoluted political diatribe. While
he considers Borges's politics to be unacceptable, he appears to respect him
for not pretending (as does the nefarious Fuentes) to be a leftist. Moreover,
Retamar firmly believes that the charges frequently leveled at Borges that he
is not "American," that he is a misplaced European, are unfounded. Rather,
he argues, "Borges is a typical colonial writer, the representative among us of
a now-powerless class for whom the act of writing . . . is more like the act of
reading . . . there is no European writer like Borges. But there are *many* European writers . . . whom Borges has *read*, shuffled together, collated. . . . there
is only one type of person who really knows in its entirety the literature of
Europe: the colonial" (*C*, 28). He goes on to characterize Borges's concept of
culture as "a library, or better yet a museum": his "elegant pages" are, in the
final analysis, "the painful testimony of a class with no way out, diminished to
saying in the voice of one man, 'The world, unfortunately, is real; I, unfortunately, am Borges' " (*C*, 29). Retamar's citation of the last line of Borges's well-
known essay "Nueva refutación del tiempo" demonstrates, in my view, how a
highly personal bit of poetic prose can be taken out of context and interpreted—or misinterpreted—as the testimony of an entire class.

An interesting by-product of Fernández Retamar's hyperideological treatment of Borges and Fuentes is his broad attack upon a major trend in literary

criticism which rightly or wrongly he associates with these writers. He claims that Fuentes, in his study of the new novel, has given insufficient attention to the reinterpretation of Latin American history as found in the *nueva narrativa* of recent decades: "Fuentes dissipates the flesh and blood of our novels . . . and, as I have said, calmly applies the schemes derived from other literatures (those of the capitalist countries), now reduced to mere linguistic speculations" (*C*, 33). These "schemes" are in effect the formalist critical approaches—structuralism, in the main—that blossomed in France during the 1950s and became widely diffused throughout the Americas shortly afterward. Retamar admits that there may indeed be valid technical reasons why these new critical approaches have enjoyed such a vogue. Yet he is quick to point out that "there are *ideological* reasons for it over and above the subject matter itself. . . . and among them is the attempt at ahistorization peculiar to a dying class: a class that initiated its trajectory with daring utopias in order to chase away time and that endeavors now, in the face of adversity, to arrest that trajectory via impossible *uchronics*" (*C*, 33). In essence Retamar holds that Latin American writers and critics who embrace structuralism and related movements are guilty of two literary crimes (or misdemeanors): that of fleeing reality for the safety of linguistic gamesmanship and, by virtue of using "systems derived from other literatures and other methodologies," of revealing "typical colonial attitudes" (*C*, 33).[16] Since my purpose here is to show how the ideological mind functions rather than to analyze the strengths and weaknesses of a particular critical viewpoint, I shall not pursue Retamar's comments on structuralism further. Moreover, it should be noted that in *Calibán* this potentially fruitful discussion soon deteriorates into literary invective directed toward those whose underlying sins, in addition to having colonial mentalities and to being associated with structuralism, include their failure to pass Retamar's litmus test of loyalty to Castro's Cuba. Consequently, in addition to his attacks upon Borges, Fuentes, and the long-dead Sarmiento, Retamar delights in aiming his darts at the late Emir Rodríguez Monegal (the Yale scholar in the pay of the CIA, he claims), at Spanish novelist Goytisolo, at the "neo-Barthean flutterings of Severo Sarduy," and at very anti-Castro Cuban exile Guillermo Cabrera Infante.

Fernández Retamar concludes *Calibán* by noting the progress of Marxism in Latin America and by reminding his readers that the new culture of the area "can only be . . . the child of revolution, of our multisecular rejection of all colonialism" (*C*, 38). In support he cites such writers as Cuba's greatest essayist, José Martí; the Peruvian radical of the 1920s, José Carlos Mariátegui; and Argentine leftist Ezéquiel Martínez Estrada, all of whom illustrate the cultural authenticity he seeks. He then returns to his reinterpretation of the Ariel-Caliban-Prospero symbology and affirms again that the intellectual community (i.e., "Ariel") "must break all ties with its class origin (frequently the bourgeoisie) and must sever the nexus of *dependence* upon the metropolitan culture from which it has learned, nonetheless, a language as well as a conceptual apparatus" (*C*, 40). Lest anyone misunderstand he rephrases his position in unequivocal terms: "the frivolous way in which some intellectuals who call themselves leftists (and who, nonetheless, don't give a damn about the masses) rush forth shamelessly to repeat word for word the same critique of the socialist world proposed and promulgated by capitalism only demonstrates that they have not broken with capitalism as radically as they might think" (*C*, 42). And as a final summation of his position he cites Fidel Castro's now famous statement regarding the limits imposed upon intellectuals in the new Cuba: "within the revolution, everything; outside the revolution, nothing. . . . to the extent that the revolution expresses the interest of the nation as a whole, [no one] can maintain any right in opposition to it" (*C*, 43).

Although the critiques of Fernández Retamar, Benedetti, and Guevara best illustrate the ideological orthodoxy of the left, other essayists of the period may be mentioned as holding essentially similar positions. Eduardo Galeano and Julio Cortázar, for example, have been staunch supporters of the Cubans, though both tend to avoid technical Marxist analyses in their work. While they have very different literary personalities, they are similar in that they may be considered "informal leftists" rather than doctrinaire ideologues. The writings of the two have already been discussed earlier in connection with the related issues of rebellion and the youth movement: their more overtly political views will be noted at this point.

Galeano comes closest to espousing a consistent ideology in his most widely discussed essay, *Las venas abiertas de América Latina*, an informal work containing texts that range from bits of highly charged invective, ironic political comment, and, on occasion, sober historical analysis. Despite this variety of authorial strategies, several interrelated ideas concerning Latin America's position vis-à-vis the developed world constitute a fairly cohesive viewpoint; namely, what students of Third World thought have termed "dependency theory." The core of this concept can be simply stated: the poverty, instability, and lack of development of Latin America is the direct result of its economic dependence upon the rich neocolonial powers, especially the United States. Or, in its briefest formulation, "we are poor because they are rich." To support his basic thesis Galeano offers considerable evidence: economic data regarding price differentials between Latin America's exported raw materials and imported manufactured goods (*VA*, 371); historical analysis of how spokesmen for the continent's mercantile cities (Sarmiento, for example) argued for free trade, thus ensuring dependency on foreign manufacturers; how Latin America has failed to develop its own internal markets; how monoculture (encouraged by foreign exploiters) cripples the economy (*VA*, 90); and how the continent's infrastructure (its rail system, for example) was planned primarily to aid the imperialists to extract the region's raw materials (*VA*, 308).[17]

These views, drawn from Galeano's own observations and from the writings of a heterodox group of nationalist/leftist authors (J. Abelardo Ramos, André Gunder Frank, Celso Furtado, René Dumont, and Darcy Ribeiro), provide a good summary of the widely held *dependista* position. However, Galeano's comments fall short of constituting a full-blown descriptive or prescriptive ideological model. He is, after all, an essayist and not a political theorist. Though he has clearly been a supporter of the Cuban revolution, it is interesting to note that he apparently does not consider the *castrista* solution of the dependency problem to be the only way of stemming the flow of blood issuing from the continent's open veins, to use his own metaphor. Rather, he sees a variety of models: these include the programs promulgated by Argentina's Juan Perón, Brazil's Getulio Vargas, Mexico's Lázaro Cárdenas, Peru's General Velasco, and, curiously, the regime of the nineteenth-century Paraguayan despot, Gaspar Rodríguez de Francia (*VA*, 291–293). His choice of the latter is revealing. Galeano holds, perhaps justifiably, that in the past century "Paraguay held itself up as an exception in Latin America: the only nation that foreign capital had not deformed" (*VA*, 292). By this he means that Francia's nationalistic (and megalomaniacal?) policy of isolation and autarchy permitted Paraguay to develop its own economy and to create a state in which "there were no great fortunes . . . [but] the only country of Latin America that did not have beggars, hungry people or thieves" (*VA*, 293). He adds that travelers also reported that all the nation's children could read and write. Whether Galeano's idyllic picture of mid-nineteenth-century Paraguay is accurate or not may be left to the experts; however, his casual dismissal of democracy in Francia's regime bears noting: "Francia had gained his support among the masses of the countryside to crush the Paraguayan oligarchy. . . . Expropriation, exile, imprisonment, persecution, and fines did not serve to consolidate the internal domination of landholders and merchants but rather . . . were used for their destruction. There did not exist, nor would there exist later, political liberties or the right of opposition; but in that historical stage only those who were nostalgic for lost privilege were bothered by the lack of democracy" (*VA*, 292–293). Galeano's enthusiasm for Francia's despotic rule suggests that he believes that virtually any leader or regime capable of asserting nationalism and putting bread on the table of the people can be excused for its suppression of political and human rights; hence his positive assessment of such authoritarian populists as Perón, Vargas, or Velasco Alvarado. Sympathetic observers might consider his ideological position as a very simple and very practical one, though others would condemn it as another blatant example of unacceptable means justifying desirable ends.

Galeano's overall attitude toward the United States is, not surprisingly, quite negative. At times his strident outcry goes beyond the usual litany of North American crimes and approaches paranoia, as when he suggests that the spreading of birth control information (through American Protestant missionaries, among others) is a thinly veiled plot to "sterilize" Latin America (*VA*, 211); or, as he states early in his book, "it is more efficient to kill guerrillas in the womb than in the sierras or city streets" (*VA*, 10). Yet beneath this surface of highly charged anti-Yankee rhetoric Galeano reveals an interesting ambiguity regarding this country in that much of what he urges Latin America to do—especially in the area of economic policy—is precisely what the United States did in the past to achieve its position of dominance. He seems to wish that Latin America would have protected its infant industries, developed internal markets, diversified its agriculture, and the like. Surprisingly he does not look to existing Marxist states—Cuba, for example—as models for hemispheric development: all this despite his frequent expressions of admiration for leaders of the extreme left and of sympathy for what may be called the mystique of Marxism.[18] In short, Galeano's "ideology" (I use the quotation marks advisedly) is an idiosyncratic mélange born of romantic hero worship, of a deep-seated desire to assert the region's nationalism, of some credible economic analysis, and of a genuine concern for the material welfare of Latin America's masses. As such, and despite its inconsistencies, it probably represents a worldview held by a goodly number of Spanish American intellectuals of the period.

Like those of Galeano, the ideological positions of the late Julio Cortázar are not particularly orthodox nor are they set forth in a coherent, organized fashion in any single text. A highly sophisticated prose writer, Cortázar shunned overt political declarations in his early novels and short stories, though in interviews and in several essayistic texts written later in his career his ideological leanings emerge quite clearly.[19] While much of Cortázar's thinking parallels that of other leftists, his strong aesthetic commitment has complicated his political position. Throughout his life he held to the view that artists—especially literary artists—should enjoy full creative freedom. Hence he abjured all heavy-handed writing that pretended to justify itself by its "message," even though as a political being he might support the views presented. Consistent with this position he was never an enthusiast for the kind of social realism encouraged by leftist regimes; rather, he believed that fully creative writers, especially innovators, could in a sense help realize Marxist objectives by dint of their revolutionary approach to literary art. Not surprisingly, this belief as well as his radical chic life-style in France were frequently questioned by his colleagues on the left.

Two texts are especially helpful as illustrative of Cortázar's ideological stance. Both may be considered essays, though the first, "Acerca de la situación del intelectual latinoamericano" (Regarding the situation of the Latin American intellectual, 1967), is cast in the form of a letter for publication, addressed to Fernández Retamar. The second, "Literatura en la revolución y revolución en la literatura" (Literature in the revolution and the revolution in literature, 1969),[20] is a reply to an essay by a leftist critic, Oscar Collazos, who questions Cortázar's legitimacy as a revolutionary writer. In both texts Cortázar's tone is defensive: in simplest terms he strives to show that he can be a devoted Marxist while maintaining his independence as an artist. Thus he states early in the letter to Retamar: "I consider myself above all to be a *cronopio* who writes stories and novels without any objective except that which is extensively pursued by all *cronopios*, that is, one's personal delight" (*UR*, pb, 200).[21] He admits in the same piece that his early life was "saturated" by bourgeois thinking, but that "more and more [I] have become deeply involved in the paths of socialism" (*UR*, pb, 208). Yet a few pages later he restates his commitment to aesthetic independence: "at the risk of disillusioning those who recite the catechism of art at the service of the masses, I continue to be that *cronopio* . . . who writes for his own enjoyment or suffering without the slightest concession, without 'Latin American' or 'socialist' obligations, understood as pragmatic a priori" (*UR*, pb, 210). However, he goes on to note that his basic problem as a human being is "a continuous tension between the monstrous error of being what we are as individuals and as nations in these times, and the glimpse of a future in which human society might become at last that archetype of which socialism provides a practical vision and poetry a spiritual vision" (*UR*, pb, 213). If we read "poetry" in the broad sense of pure literary creativity it becomes apparent that Cortázar has attempted to reconcile the problem of art versus political commitment by clinging to the notion that both are paths leading toward a utopian blossoming of humanity.

In the second text, the response to Collazos's essay, Cortázar is even more defensive. Collazos had charged that the new novelists, the celebrated "boom" writers (Fuentes, Vargas Llosa, and Cortázar himself), were producing novels "radically distanced from reality" and in which language enjoyed a kind of autonomous existence. The Colombian critic implied that artists like Cortázar often proclaim their allegiance to the left but in their own work are unwilling to sacrifice their aesthetic independence. In short, Collazos attacked Cortázar and others for embracing the traditional art-for-art's-sake position rather than one of political commitment. He even cited a passage in *La vuelta al día en ochenta mundos* (Around the day in eighty worlds, 1967), in which Cortázar ridicules leftist café intellectuals who insist on "being authentic" and "facing up to reality" but who are only using the rhetoric of commitment to mask the inferiority of their own literary efforts (*LR*, 14). Among Cortázar's transgressions, Collazos maintained, is "to authorize, 'legalize' . . . this excision of the political being from the literary being" (*LR*, 15). He also attacked Cortázar for aping European literary fads—a sign of a "colonial" mentality—and above all for not transcribing the Latin American situation in realistic terms.

In his reply Cortázar takes up all these charges; however, he is most eloquent in defending himself as a realist, but a realist in his own terms. What Collazos and others who have a simplistic view of literary realism have not understood is that "all prose based upon *sympathy* (that is, upon a spiritual, intuitive, magical, or mythic grasp of the analogies and resonances of the reality of human consciousness) carries within itself a hidden aspect charged with potentialities, symmetries, polarities . . . in which resides the justification (that is, the profound reality) of great literature" (*LR*, 48). Cortázar further attacks his opponent's concept of reality as being too firmly rooted in "concrete" or "sociocultural" considerations. In short, he finds Collazos actually defending orthodox social realism, though the Colombian critic refrains from using this discredited term.

Later in his essay Cortázar defends his highly experimental novel, *62: modelo para armar* (*62: A Model Kit*, 1968), against the charge that it is trivial, escapist, and unworthy of an author who espouses revolutionary Marxism. His refutation gets to the very heart of the problem faced by writers who are politically committed but who wish to work untrammeled by the straitjacket of social realism: "revolutionary novels are not only those that have a revolutionary 'content' but rather those that attempt to revolutionize the novel itself, the form of the novel" (*LR*, 73). In sum, Cortázar believed, rightly or wrongly, that the production of innovative, avant garde literature would, perhaps by jarring readers away from traditional ways of viewing reality, further the cause of political revolution. This basic notion is set forth in a dramatic statement at the conclusion of the essay: "one of the most critical Latin American problems is that now more than ever we need the Che Guevaras of language, *revolutionaries of literature more than literati of the revolution*" (*LR*, 76). To what extent Cortázar was himself a "revolutionary of literature," and especially of the essay, will be considered in our final chapter.

THE DOUBTERS

Although unorthodox in their thinking, writers such as Galeano and Cortázar maintained their loyalty to Cuba and the socialist world through the 1970s and into the 1980s. However, at the same time a number of other essayists, representing various shadings of leftist ideology, were distancing themselves from existing Marxist regimes, especially that of Castro's Cuba. In some cases this process paralleled a worldwide movement which had its roots in the early disillusionment experienced by idealistic Marxists in the face of the repressive Soviet regime of the 1930s and 1940s. In other cases Latin American writers reacted directly to the growing trend toward bureaucratization, personalism, and conformity of the Castro government, especially after the Padilla affair. Finally, a few essayists (Paz is perhaps the best example) sensed at an early date that the Marxist world, on both a practical and ideological level, was approaching a crisis, a presentiment amply confirmed by recent events.

Argentina's Ernesto Sábato (1911–) would appear to belong to the generation that preceded most of the writers considered in this study. Yet Sábato has continued to produce essays (and novels) well into the period under consideration and in addition has played a significant role in the affairs of his country.[22] Most important, he represents the kind of classic Latin American leftist whose loyalty to Marxism was first established through an appreciation of the French literary left (Sartre, Malraux, and others), who later was an admirer of the Cuban revolution (especially of Che Guevara), but who gradually came to realize that the Castro regime, like earlier communist experiments, had fallen far short of the utopia sought by the Marxist visionaries. Like his Peruvian colleague, Mario Vargas Llosa, Sábato views the role of a writer as essentially that of a perennial *rebelde*. In his essay collection *El escritor y sus fantasmas* (The writer and his phantoms, 1963) he states this position very clearly: "the writer of profound fiction is at heart . . . a rebel, and therefore he frequently is a fellow traveler of revolutionary movements. But when [the] revolutionaries triumph, it is not unusual for him to be a rebel again."[23] It is perhaps consistent with this view that Sábato has not been especially effusive in his praise of Fidel Castro; yet he could write glowingly of Che Guevara on the occasion of the latter's death, an event which may be seen as romantically symbolizing an unsuccessful revolution.[24]

By the early seventies Sábato's position on Cuba and the *castrista* version of Marxism became even clearer. In his *Claves políticas* (Political keys, 1971)—actually a published debate between Sábato and a group of writers representing Argentina's younger leftists—he notes his support of Cuba and his opposition to the Bay of Pigs invasion, but he also expresses grave concerns regarding the dangers of one-party government.[25] It was because he could not support the Cubans unconditionally that he refused on several occasions to accept their invitations to visit the island and participate in government-sponsored literary competitions. Of course, like many one-time communist sympathizers the world over, Sábato admits that his disenchantment with Marxist regimes had begun much earlier, in the days of the Stalinist terror.[26]

Sábato, however, has not been an unreserved admirer of free enterprise democracies. For one thing, he finds the highly developed (Western) world to be what he calls "a model for disaster." By this he means that the West's "technolatry"—the worship of material progress—has created superstates that repress, exploit, and dehumanize:

> Massification suppresses individual desires or tries to do this, because the Superstate needs everyone to be the same. In the best of cases it will collectivize desires and massify instincts, it will build huge stadiums to convert [desires] into a single shout, it will dull sensibilities by means of television, it will homogenize taste by means of propaganda and slogans, it will favor a kind of all-encompassing, mechanized, single-minded dream of people leaving factories and offices, where they are slaves of computers and machines, to enter the domain of mass sports or the illusory realm of mechanically produced stories and entertainment.[27]

Although Sábato believes that both the Marxist East and the capitalist West have been guilty of creating alienating superstates, he recognizes an all-important difference in the Western nations. Despite the fact that greed, egoism, and the thirst for power may corrupt democratic societies, in countries such as Britain, France, and the United States deeply ingrained institutions exist which mitigate evils of human nature and the potential excesses of government. In this regard he singles out such things as the division of powers and, most important, the guarantees of free expression and of the right to dissent. Sábato is especially eloquent in his praise of the United States in these areas. Speaking of Latin America in general and of Argentina in particular he states, "We are rarely inclined to recognize in the United States one of the greatest spiritual values, which in practice we generally ignore or even prohibit: the capacity for self-criticism and the incorruptible right of dissent. Like every great empire it has committed innumerable outrages throughout the world. But no one has spoken more harshly of the United States than its own children." Toward the end of the same essay Sábato sums up his position: "in short, democracy is precarious and at times despicable, but until now we haven't found anything better to achieve the future community to which we aspire."[28]

Considerable Spanish American criticism of the communist world has come from within the ranks of the left—from writers who, while mercilessly attacking existing regimes such as Cuba or the former Soviet Union, profess allegiance to some form of Marxist faith. Often such individuals hold to idiosyncratic or simply unorthodox positions: they are the true believers whose self-defined ideological purity separates them from both the conventional anti-Marxists and the supporters of existing communist parties. A typical case of this kind of thinking may be found in the political essays of Sábato's countryman, J. J. Sebreli. For example, in his *Tercer mundo, mito burgués*, a work cited in an earlier chapter, Sebreli sets forth the idea that the Soviet and Cuban regimes consti- tute little more than "bureaucratic state capitalism," that the only "honest" radicals were Trotsky or Che Guevara, and that Castro, Stalin, and the present- day Soviets were "compromisers" (*TMM*, 201–218). Sebreli's criticism of the Cubans is especially vitriolic: Castro, in his words, is a "typical petit bourgeois Jacobin" (*TMM*, 226) who has built his regime upon the manipulation of un- sophisticated masses ill-prepared for a genuine revolution. In Sebreli's rather bookish view, the absence of leadership by an organized, revolutionary working class makes the Cuban experiment unauthentic: "the Cuban revolution is only doing the tasks that the Cuban bourgeoisie should have done a century earlier . . . In reality, *castrismo* is a form of twentieth-century Jacobinism, that is, a radicalized party of the petit bourgeoisie which, in the name of the people, has proposed a bourgeois revolution . . . Castro got his support from the rural masses. The working class did not play any leading role, thus demonstrating *castrismo*'s petit bourgeois character" (*TMM*, 223). It is curious to read Sebreli's litany of *castrista* "errors" against Marxist orthodoxy, ranging from the fact that the working class did not achieve its own emancipation to the regime's general disregard of theory. In short, Sebreli decries the fact that Castro proceeded pragmatically, that he "denied the Marxist-Leninist thesis according to which 'there can be no revolutionary action without revolutionary theory' " (*TMM*, 230). We have already noted how Sebreli criticizes the Cuban state, as well as the Chinese and the Soviets, for imposing censorship, police terror, and the abrogation of civil rights in their pursuit of development.[29] And, in an essay published in 1976, he takes the interesting position that "a genuine philo- sophic consideration of Marxism can only be undertaken outside of the self- proclaimed Marxist parties and groups where freedom of investigation, of ex- pression, of criticism, of discussion have been substituted by the principle of authority, and where the cynicism of the directing demagogue corresponds symmetrically with the stupidity of the mass of devout militants."[30] While he refuses to admit that he had abandoned his fundamental Marxist ideology, by 1983 Sebreli's position was one of firm support for the newly elected liberal democratic regime of Alfonsín. His point in lending this support is that, unlike the Peronists or the military, the new president and his party offer "the political space where social democracy might emerge following the European pattern, which in turn might provide conditions for the emergence of a new left" (*RP*, 209). In the same text he states that were he a European he would not hesitate to vote for Mitterand or for Felipe González's moderate socialism (*RP*, 208). In short, after years of devotion to revolutionary Marxism, after examining the course of existing communist regimes, after considering the alternative offered by Peronism and the military, Sebreli opts for moderately progressive regimes that are essentially pragmatic rather than ideological in their approach to problems. His lip service to his one-time infatuation with Marxism remains vaguely in the background; but it reminds one of an aging man's dream that a youthful love affair will somehow be reborn.

A sense that ideology in general and Marxism in particular were waning becomes abundantly evident among other Spanish American writers by the early 1970s. Understandably this trend was underscored by the growing rift between the intellectuals and Castro's Cuba. In few writers is this more evident than in the work of Chile's Jorge Edwards, one of that country's most distinguished short story writers and an essayist of considerable talent. Like Sábato, Sebreli, and many others, Edwards had been a Marxist sympathizer and, in the early years, an enthusiastic admirer of Fidel Castro. In 1970 his support of Allende, the newly elected communist president, gained him the post of Chilean chargé d'affaires in Havana with the mission of reopening his country's embassy on the island. Previously he had visited Cuba as a guest of the official publishing house, Casa de las Américas, had written in several Cuban literary journals, and had joined pro-Castro intellectuals in protesting Yankee intervention in the Caribbean.[31] Despite these politically correct credentials Edwards had considerable misgivings about accepting the Cuban post. He knew that some of his Cuban friends—writers Padilla and Arrufat, especially— were under criticism by the government; he knew too that the fact that some of the wealthy Edwards family were notoriously conservative mitigated against him being fully accepted by the left. Finally, he knew that important people in his own government had advised Allende against sending him to Cuba. This web of circumstance makes *Persona non grata* (1973) a fascinating and unusual text. Written in an informal first person, it is an essay only in the broadest sense: Edwards himself calls it a "rediscovered genre" consisting of "rambling memoirs, part literary and part political" (*PNG*, 1). What makes it especially intriguing, however, are the author's constant doubts and suspicions regarding his relationship to both the Cuban regime and his own government. In Edwards's terms, the book is "an effort of memory not too far removed from the methods of psychoanalysis" (*PNG*, 31).

The strongest points made by Edwards concern the insistence upon conformity and the atmosphere of repression created by the Cuban leadership. In his interview with Prime Minister Raúl Roa he senses that this highly placed intellectual was extremely suspicious of Edwards's "questioning way of tackling problems" and his "rejection of dogmatism" (*PNG*, 32). And in his conference with Fidel himself, apropos of Padilla and other dissidents, he notes the Cuban leader's complete rejection of dissent: "he did not think that a better, more humane socialism might emerge from the act of criticizing" (*PNG*, 152). He goes on to observe that despite his purported open political style Castro probably feels more at home with authoritarian figures, with the "power international," with a Brezhnev or even a Western president than he does with "poets and intellectuals, who are essentially intransigent and unaccommodating beings" (*PNG*, 165).

References to the Eastern European bloc and parallels between Cuba and other communist regimes appear occasionally in *Persona non grata*. However, in Edwards's later collection of essays, *Desde la cola del dragón* (From the dragon's tail, 1977) these concerns become central. Of even greater interest is Edwards's growing conviction that Western intellectuals had become complacent in their uncritical acceptance of what he terms "theoretical schemes and formal elegance."[32] Furthermore, like Sebreli and others, by the late 1970s he approvingly takes note of the "leftist pluralism" emerging in countries like Spain. This support of more pragmatic, less ideological regimes is underscored by his frequent attacks on the earlier intransigence of the Chilean left, himself included—an attitude, he feels, which served only to undermine the Allende regime and to help pave the way for Pinochet and the reactionaries (*DC*, 146). Finally, with regard to his own changing views and to events throughout the world, he casually observes that many "believe that we are witnessing the twilight of ideologies" (*DC*, 149).

Edwards dedicates the final chapters of *Desde la cola del dragón* to the perennial question of the writer's role as a political being. As might be expected, he traces this concern to Sartre and specifically to his fundamental work *What Is Literature?*, the book that made an entire generation of writers, Latin Americans included, acutely aware of "commitment." Interestingly, these chapters are personalized rather than abstract: Edwards recalls a tour of Peru he undertook late in 1969 in the company of novelist Vargas Llosa during which the two were repeatedly questioned about their ideas concerning the proper stance of intellectuals in a revolutionary world. Like his Peruvian colleague, Edwards was disturbed by the fact that many of the questioners wanted stock answers expressing unconditional support of leftist regimes, especially that of Castro. His reaction to all this is stated with utmost clarity: "what is happening now, like in periods of the most primitive Manichaeism, is that the concepts of conformism and commitment have become confused. The commitment of the creative person has come to be identified with its antipode: submission to another bureaucracy and another form of censorship. . . . Authentic commitment implies intellectual risk-taking and, in cases of extreme crises, physical risk. . . . The unbending, stiffened, brittle 'compromises' of the commissars, by contrast, based on a mixture of servility and pessimism and an assimilation of past doctrines, fixed by exegetes with dogmatic validity . . . leads precisely to the perpetuation of arbitrariness" (*DC*, 164).

Edwards's companion in the 1969 tour, Mario Vargas Llosa (1934–   ), is thought of primarily as one of contemporary Spanish America's most distinguished novelists. However, like Fuentes or Cortázar, Vargas is a superb writer of essayistic prose. Indeed, had he never produced such masterworks as *La casa verde, Conversación en la catedral,* or *La guerra del fin del mundo,* it is quite conceivable that he would have gained recognition as a cultural commentator, political essayist, and literary critic. His collected work in these areas fills several volumes and, most important, provides a remarkable overview not only of his own ideological trajectory but also that of numerous intellectuals of his generation.[33] Thus in addition to his being a kind of barometer of the ideas and issues dominating the essay of 1960 to 1985, Vargas's specific positions regarding dissent and ideology make his work central to this study.

The title of his first collection, *Entre Sartre y Camus* (Between Sartre and Camus, 1981), is significant in that it points up a fruitful polarity in his thinking. For the youthful Vargas Llosa (the essays collected here go back to the early 1960s), the two French writers represent, on the one hand, rationalism, man as an urban creature, a product of history (Sartre); and, on the other, man as irrational, shaped by the world of nature, an ahistoric "outsider" (Camus). As a young Latin American with a strong affinity for European culture but also with a kind of Third World outlook, not unlike that of the Franco-Algerian Camus, Vargas often finds himself figuratively positioned somewhere between his two mentors. Closer examination, however, reveals that the ideas of Sartre weigh somewhat more heavily in his own thinking. Two clusters of issues raised by the latter appear frequently and persistently in the Peruvian's work: questions revolving about *engagement* (a writer's political, if not revolutionary, obligations) and the Sartrean view that formal liberal democracy without socioeconomic justice was in fact false democracy. In the collections following, *Contra viento y marea* (Against wind and tide, 1983) and *Contra viento y marea II* (Against wind and tide II, 1986), Vargas continues to probe these issues along with many others: the pernicious effects of censorship; the immorality of international terrorism; problems of education, especially in the university; the dangers of ideological orthodoxy; the critique of the United States's policy in Latin America; the growing force of statism, especially in the Soviet bloc and Cuba; and, of course, his ceaseless pursuit of basic literary questions.

"My disillusionment with Sartre occurred in the summer of 1964," writes Vargas, "upon reading an article that he had written in *Le Monde* in which he seemed to renounce everything that he had believed—and had made us believe—regarding literature. He said that confronted by a starving child, *La náusea* was useless, was worthless. Did this mean that writing novels or poems was pointless, or, even worse, immoral while social injustice existed? Apparently yes, for in the same piece he advised writers of the new African countries to give up writing for the time being and dedicate themselves to teaching and more urgent tasks."[34] In the essay just cited, "The Mandarin," Vargas confesses that he felt "betrayed" by the man who had earlier taught that literature was tremendously important and that it could in fact influence and modify the real world. In a companion text, "Sartre twenty years later," he notes that in the late 1940s and early 1950s he carried a copy of Sartre's *What Is Literature?* as a kind of vade mecum when as a member of the university's Fracción Universitaria Comunista he tried to refute arguments regarding literature proffered by his more orthodox Marxist comrades (*ESC*, 109). These essays—and several others on related themes—make it clear that while Vargas appreciated Sartre's early concept of literary engagement, even as a young militant he rejected the notion of literature at the service of revolution or the state. By the 1960s he refers to his early devotion to Sartre as something that he now views with "nostalgia and surprise" (*ESC*, 109).

Vargas Llosa's understanding of engagement, of the writer's social and political commitment, was evolving along slightly different lines. For him, literary activity by its very nature stems from a sense of disconformity between an author and the world about him: it is as if authentic writers were condemned—to use a Sartrean term—to a kind of restless and continuous criticism of reality. This idea appears frequently in his essays of the 1960s and beyond, but one of its most eloquent formulations is found in "La literatura es fuego" (Literature is fire), the published text of his speech upon receiving the prestigious Rómulo Gallegos literary prize in the summer of 1967: "there is no escape: writers have been, are, and will keep on being malcontents. No one who is satisfied is capable of writing, no one who is in agreement, who is reconciled with reality, will commit the pretentious folly of inventing verbal realities. Literary vocation is born of the disagreement between a man and the world . . . Literature is a form of permanent insurrection which tolerates no straitjackets . . . Literature may die but it will never be conformist."[35] He continues by noting that only by fulfilling this role will literature be useful to society and that the more merciless a writer is in criticizing his own country, the stronger will be the bonds that unite him to the *patria*.

This position exalting the writer as the archetypal voice of dissent obviously led Vargas to take an unequivocal stand against all forms of censorship, overt forms of thought control, and even more subtle pressures for conformity, as those that might be exercised by one's peers or by nongovernmental institutions such as the university. As we shall see, these preoccupations dominate a number of the essays in these collections. Toward the end of the 1960s and into succeeding decades Vargas found not only the right but also the left increasingly guilty of exercising various forms of thought control. However, in the 1967 text just cited he still maintains a remarkably positive evaluation on the present achievements and future possibilities of socialism.[36] After noting that injustice has been and continues to be widespread in many parts of Latin America he observes that "within ten, twenty, or perhaps fifty years the hour of social justice will probably arrive, as it has already in Cuba, and all of Latin America will have freed itself of the empire that loots it, the castes that exploit it, and the forces that offend and repress it today. I desire this time to come as soon as possible and that Latin America should, once and for all, enjoy dignity and modernity [and] that socialism should rid us of our anachronisms and horrors" (*CVM*, 135). Vargas's comments following this forthright endorsement of the left and of Cuban socialism must, however, be carefully considered in the light of a qualification he expresses immediately afterward: "but even when social injustice disappears, the time for writers to give consent, to subordinate themselves, or to grant complicity will in no way have arrived. Their mission will continue to be, must be, the same; any compromise in this area constitutes, on the part of writers, a betrayal. Within the new society . . . we will have to continue . . . saying no, being rebels, demanding that our right to dissent be recognized" (*CVM*, 136). Of course, even earlier Vargas had expressed this view, so central to his thinking. In an article protesting the Soviet persecution of two writers (Andrei Sinionski and Yule Daniel) accused of satirizing the state, he noted that "we writers who believe in socialism and who consider ourselves friends of the Soviet Union should be the first to protest and in the most energetic terms" (*CVM*, 85). It is of some significance that during this period Vargas Llosa continues to reaffirm his allegiance to socialism, yet he repeatedly states his view that "the socialism we desire not only will have done away with the exploitation of man, but it will also have suppressed the final obstacles for writers to write freely about whatever they choose, beginning, naturally, with their hostility toward socialism itself" (*CVM*, 102).

This position was soon to be put to the test. Vargas, in addition to attacking the suppression of free speech in the U.S.S.R., was becoming increasingly critical of the Cubans. In the same 1970 polemic in which Cortázar and Oscar Collazos crossed swords,[37] Vargas published a stinging defense of the right to dissent and also a sharp rebuke of Fidel Castro, who had supported the Soviet invasion of Czechoslovakia. It is a tribute to the probity of the Peruvian that at approximately the same time he could also write another piece criticizing the United States for its military suppression of a left-of-center revolution in the Dominican Republic: "the sending of Soviet tanks to Prague to liquidate by force a movement for the democratization of socialism is not as reprehensible as sending the U.S. Marines to Santo Domingo to violently squelch a popular uprising against a military dictatorship and a system of social injustice" (*CVM*, 160). But the issue which was to tip the scales against the left for Vargas and many other Latin Americans was the hotly debated Padilla affair. Heberto Padilla, a Cuban writer of considerable talent, had since 1967 been involved in a series of skirmishes with the *castrista* literary establishment, the details of which need not concern us here.[38] At any rate, in March 1970 Padilla was imprisoned for about seven weeks: shortly before being released he signed a lengthy statement of self-criticism in which he "confessed" to a number of counter-revolutionary literary activities which he subsequently read at an opening meeting of the National Union of Writers and Artists (UNEAC). Latin American writers and intellectuals as well as others throughout the world decried the Cubans' manipulation of the situation. To many it seemed very likely that the prison "confession" had been forced in an atmosphere reminiscent of the worst days of the early Soviet dictatorship. There were two letters of protest signed by a long list of distinguished people:[39] the first was rather mild but the second was outspoken in likening the Castro regime's operations to the tactics of Stalinist terror. Vargas Llosa—unlike Cortázar and García Márquez, both of whom supported only the first letter—signed both. At the same time he sent a strong note to Haydée Santamarina, then the *directora* of the official government publishing house, Casa de las Américas, in which he severed connections with that entity. He also accused the Cubans of forcing Padilla's confession by "methods repugnant to human dignity" and of committing acts that constituted "the negation of what made me embrace the cause of the Cuban revolution at its very inception: its decision to fight for social justice without losing its respect for the individual." He ends this bristling text on an ironic note: "I know that this letter may occasion invectives against me: they will not be worse than those I have merited for having defended Cuba" (*CVM*, 165). And, in June 1971, just a few months after this apparent break with Cuban officialdom, Vargas could say, in an interview published in the Peruvian weekly *Caretas*, "Let no one be fooled: with all its errors, the Cuban revolution is even today the most just society of Latin America and to defend it against its enemies is for me a pressing and honorable obligation" (*CVM*, 172).

Earlier I noted that Vargas Llosa may be considered a barometer of the thinking and attitudes of Latin American writers of the period. His political position in the early 1970s bears this out: like a number of others, for example, Jorge Edwards and Octavio Paz, both of whom he cites approvingly, he was at a crossroads regarding ideology and the Marxist world. He apparently still considered such things as the Soviet repression in Czechoslovakia or Hungary and the Cuban restraint of free expression as "exceptions" or "deviations" from an otherwise admirable sociopolitical system. But soon he would modify this ambiguous stance and in the process would come to doubt the efficacy of ideology itself.

Closely related to these issues in his essays is his constant challenging of intellectual conformity, of those inflexible attitudes toward open discussion and dissent that in later decades have come to be called "political correctness." An obvious locus of his concern are governments—any governments—that attempt to stifle free expression. Thus he forthrightly protested the specious rationale of Peruvian authorities for shutting down opposition publications in the name of "socializing" the media for the benefit of the people. In his unequivocal essay of 1978, "Libertad de información y derecho de crítica" (Freedom of information and the right to criticize), he makes his position clear:

There is not a single case in modern history of a society in which, once the State has taken control of the means of communication, freedom of information and criticism of power have survived. This holds for fascist regimes, for the Marxists, and for those hybrids of the two which proliferate in the Third World. It doesn't matter in the name of which ideology the state control is carried out: Nasserism, African nationalism . . . Maoism, Francoism, the "society of self-managing full participation" (General Velasco's formulation), Leninism, Fidelismo, Peronism, and so on. Once the state . . . gets its hands on the press, radio, and television (always with the same argument: to turn them over to the "national majority" or the "organized populace") the result is identical. (*CVM*, 290–291)

Consistent with this view, he finds the existence of privately operated media in certain countries (France, the United States, Britain, Venezuela, Israel) to provide a genuine guarantee of free speech. Of course, he realizes that newspapers such as the *New York Times*, *Le Monde*, or even a Latin American daily like *El Nacional* of Caracas cannot be free in any absolute sense—they may have a policy or "line" set by their owners and they often let the desires of their advertisers slant their presentation of certain issues. Yet they permit individual journalists to express opposing editorial views and to pursue potentially explosive lines of investigation. In support, he cites several examples: the *Washington Post*'s uncovering of the Watergate scandal and the exposé of the racist activities of an important British state corporation by a small radical London weekly (*CVM*, 293). Such cases illustrate the important point that genuine free speech must permit the expression of a full gamut of ideological positions. Vargas concludes by defying anyone to offer similar examples from any country where so often this "much reviled free enterprise in the area of information" does not exist.

Among those Latin American institutions that, despite their traditional commitment to free inquiry, have frequently been bastions of conformity are the universities. During the 1960s and early 1970s this was especially so; moreover, in the vast majority of cases the "politically correct" student position tended markedly to the left, was unreservedly pro-Castro, and was firmly anti-Yankee. By his own confession Vargas Llosa himself fit this student stereotype in his youth (*CVM*, 382). By the late 1970s, however, he had become increasingly critical of the radical chic atmosphere pervading student groups as well as many faculty offices. We have already noted the same critical view in Carlos Rangel's sly comment that "to be a 'revolutionary' in a Latin American university is more or less as heterodox and as risky as being a fervent Catholic in an Irish seminary."[40] In a similar vein, Vargas finds that as scholasticism enjoyed a privileged position as *the* dogma in the medieval university, so Marxism enjoys an unassailable ideological position on today's campus (*CVM*, 341). In a series of essays written in 1979, he finds, moreover, the nation's leading public universities to be "bitter enemies of culture" where those "who dare to speak . . . of freedom of the press or representative democracy as civilized forms of life . . . run the risk of being considered agents of the CIA" (*CVM*, 338–339). He is especially critical of the professors (the so-called progressive intellectuals), whom he accuses of being cowardly and manipulative: "if fanaticism and narrow dogmatism become firmly rooted in the classroom, it will no longer be a place for any kind of creative, unconventional thinking. In such an atmosphere those who have their own ideas must disguise them and limit themselves to reciting the Marxist catechism in its most rudimentary (but most noisy) form" (*CVM*, 339). It is important to note, however, that Vargas does not restrict his attack to those public institutions where the left holds sway: he also observes that Peruvian private schools and universities do little more than prepare future administrators and that the military academies specialize in producing future dictators.

In his extensive essay "Reflexiones sobre una moribunda" (Reflections on a dying being, 1979), Vargas Llosa discussed a broad range of issues dealing with the present state of Latin American universities, though his focus remains on Peruvian institutions. He acknowledges the positive effects of the widespread university reform movement of the early 1920s; however, he points out that certain facets of that movement have raised false hopes or, in some cases, have led to a serious displacement of the university's primary mission. The laudable objective of providing a free education for all qualified students, for example, has been difficult to carry out: more often than not in relatively poor nations such as Peru it has only been accomplished at the cost of physical facilities, academic salaries, and so on. Closely related to the matter of opening the doors of the university to all socioeconomic classes is the question of selectivity. While Vargas certainly favors this policy, he fears that its careless implementation could lead to a lowering of standards. Thus he denies that his position is "elitist" in any negative sense when he insists upon maintaining academic quality along with providing equal opportunity for all (*CVM*, 368). But perhaps the most telling effect of the *reforma universitaria* was that in the name of modernizing the universities and making them more interactive with society as a whole, the young rebels of the 1920s called for political commitment and outreach to the masses as basic functions of institutions of higher learning. While Vargas Llosa, never a champion of the ivory tower, supports this idea, he feels that it has gotten completely out of hand so that political action has now become the primary objective of many Latin American universities. In such an environment, the real business of the university—the free, untrammeled pursuit of knowledge—has been forgotten or forced underground. Vargas makes his position very clear in his attack upon Brazilian radical sociologist Darcy Ribeiro, who, at the behest of the Velasco regime, had published a study of Peruvian higher education in which he defines the university's mission as "to carry on the revolutionary process already under way, anticipating within the university new forms of social structuring which should in the future be extended to all society" (*CVM*, 362). In his rejection of the Brazilian's views, Vargas replies in unambiguous terms: "a university stops functioning when it ceases doing what it was born to do. . . . the preservation, creation, and transmission of culture" (*CVM*, 362).

In a related essay, "El intelectual barato" (The intellectural sellout), Vargas Llosa launches a merciless attack upon writers, academics, journalists, and other members of the intellectual community who have been politicized and even "bureaucratized" by partisan movements as well as by specific political regimes. He is particularly concerned about the attempts of Peru's pseudo-leftist Velasco dictatorship to co-opt the nation's intelligentsia, though he does note other countries, such as Mexico, where the image of the idealistic, independent, "morally lucid" intellectual has been tarnished by self-interest, the desire for acceptance, and, most of all, by the opportunity—rare for the intellectual—to exercise power (*CVM*, 335). What disturbs Vargas Llosa most about those whom he ironically dubs "the progressive intellectuals" are their superficial Marxist rhetoric, their reflex action anti-Yankeeism, and their overriding hypocrisy:

> Although it is rare that they are actually members of a revolutionary party and fulfill the obligations of militancy, they are self-defined Marxists and on all occasions proclaim their conviction that North American imperialism . . . is the source of our underdevelopment. They have a good nose for sniffing out the agents of the CIA whose tentacles they even see in boy scout camps, in the tours of the Boston Symphony, or in the cartoons of Walt Disney and in everything that casts any doubt about the state-controlled economies and the rule of the single party as a social panacea. At the same time that they pollute the air of their country with these proclamations, they are candidates for Guggenheim or Rockefeller grants (which they almost always get) and when they are exiled by native dictatorships . . . it is useless to look for them in those countries that they admire and suggest as models— Cuba, China, or the U.S.S.R.—since where they invariably go to continue their revolutionary struggle is to universities such as Chicago, New York, California, and Texas, where they are "visiting professors" in hopes of being tenured. (*CVM*, 336)

Vargas Llosa feels that the presence of this kind of Latin American intellectual in Europe and in the United States has helped perpetuate an ingenuous, romanticized myth of the picturesque, essentially good Latin American humiliated and reduced to poverty by the exploiters from the developed world. Following a line of reasoning somewhat similar to what we have already seen in Rangel's *Del buen salvaje al buen revolucionario*, Vargas argues that part of the reason for this is a "phenomenon of *transference* so frequently found in European intellectuals who, while maintaining that they are interested in Latin America, are in reality interested in a fictitious Latin America, upon which they have projected those ideological appetites that their own nations cannot realize" (*CVM*, 343). Vargas notes that while some of these foreign observers may be well intentioned, they are often painfully ignorant of such basics as Latin American geography, not to mention the social and cultural complexity of the region. In some cases, sophisticated Europeans look upon the Latino intellectual as an amusing phenomenon: he must fit their stereotype of the intensely radical, hopefully bearded representative of the Third World. In addition, the Old World sophisticates underscore their essentially superior attitude by never challenging the banal rhetoric of these picturesque types when they invite them to speak at international meetings or conferences. Vargas concludes by recalling a story about certain eighteenth-century European aristocrats who "would bring monkeys from Africa to their fiestas, to satisfy their thirst for the exotic and because comparing themselves with these hairy acrobats, they felt more beautiful" (*CVM*, 344).

It would be inaccurate to state that during the 1970s Vargas Llosa was simply abandoning his early leftist positions for the ideology of conservatism and the right, though some observers have suggested this. His hard-hitting critique of Latin American leftist intellectuals stems not only from their subservience to Marxist orthodoxy and from their personal hypocrisy, but also from his growing doubts regarding the efficacy of ideology—any ideology—to apprehend reality and resolve problems. This attitude is underscored by his remarks in a 1977 review of a book dealing with the new Spanish Eurocommunism: "I have become more skeptical or, better stated, more eclectic in political matters. True solutions of major problems, it seems to me, will never be 'ideological,' that is, products of an apocalyptic reordering of society, but rather [they will be] basically pragmatic, partial, progressive; a continuous process of improvement and reform, as has been achieved in those most livable (or least unlivable) countries of the world: those democracies of the North, for example, whose inoffensive progress is not capable of exciting the enthusiasm of the intellectuals" (*CVM*, 278–279). In another text, written a year later, he again stresses his eclecticism regarding political systems. While noting his "deception" regarding Marxism and his "almost complete disagreement with the Marxist vision of man and society" (*CVM*, 288), he nonetheless points out that certain achievements of socialist countries—in such areas as literacy, public health, education, and the diffusion of culture—are admirable and could well serve as models for countries such as Peru (*CVM*, 289). Yet in the same piece he is uncompromising in his rejection of the censorship practiced in the communist bloc; moreover, he again makes clear that he cannot accept the view that the restraint of criticism can be considered simply a "deviation" or temporary "deformation" of genuine Marxist doctrine. Rather, he feels, it is *inherent* in this doctrine; "I believe that the practice of censorship . . . is an unavoidable, automatic, inescapable consequence of the axioms of Marxist theory: the so-called 'socialization' of the means of production . . . which is always translated into something which in practice should be called 'statification' " (*CVM*, 290).

Vargas Llosa's rejection of ideology was now becoming a dominant motif in his essayistic work. In an eloquent text (delivered in 1978 as his acceptance speech upon being awarded the Latin American Jewish Congress's annual prize for the defense of human rights), he strikes out again at the ideologues of the left for seeing only what they wish to see—the atrocities of the United States during the Vietnam War—but all the while ignoring the genocide practiced by the communist government of Cambodia or the aggression of Vietnam against its neighbors (*CVM*, 312). He finds that at the root of this indefensible and hypocritical attitude lies inflexible ideological loyalty: "a good part of the blame is due to those abstract formulations called ideologies, schemes to which the ideologue endeavors to reduce society, although for everything to fit neatly, it may be necessary to pulverize reality" (*CVM*, 313). To clarify his point, Vargas draws upon an old mentor: "Camus has already said it all: the only morality capable of making the world livable is that which is willing to sacrifice ideas whenever they are in opposition to life, even if it is the life of a single individual; because the latter will always be infinitely more valuable than ideas, in whose name, as we are fully aware, one can always justify, . . . with unimpeachable theory, horrible crimes" (*CVM*, 313). He then offers a rich sampling of horrors, historical as well as contemporary, that have been perpetrated in the name of political and religious ideology. Toward the end of his text he suggests that the dangers of ideology might be mitigated by a fresh look at language, "which, as we have been taught, serves to let people understand each other and to draw them together—[but] now seems to draw them apart and block communication" (*CVM*, 318). He thus considers it urgent to "reinvent political language, by cleansing it of the dross that has clogged it [and] to get it down from nebulous abstraction where it has been wandering in order to root it in the concrete experience of life" (*CVM*, 318). In short, he would purge language of all those generalizations, rhetorical flourishes, and overused labels so dear to the ideologue. He concludes by restating his basic position: "it is a question . . . after all, of admitting that neither now nor ever before has any ideology been able to capture completely within its net the complexity of human reality, and that all of them—some in a criminal fashion, others innocently—have been inescapable or, at best, insufficient to put an end to society's suffering. It's not a matter of putting all ideologues in the same basket . . . But not one has been sufficient to unequivocally show how to eradicate permanently the injustice that has accompanied humanity like a shadow since the dawn of history" (*CVM*, 320–321).

By the 1980s Vargas Llosa's eclectic political position was becoming increasingly clear. His long essay in praise of British thinker Isaiah Berlin sheds considerable light on certain apparent dichotomies which he has come to accept but which more ideological thinkers would find uncomfortable.[41] The central issue in the Berlin essay is the latter's definition of two kinds of liberty: "negative" liberty and "positive" liberty. The former is in essence the position of classical nineteenth-century liberalism and in its most extreme form is rather similar to the tenets of the present-day "libertarian" movement: "the less authority that is imposed upon my conduct, the more my behavior results from my own motivations—my needs, ambitions, personal fantasies; without interference from another's will, the freer will I be. . . . Those who defend this notion of freedom always see the greatest danger in power and authority, and thus they propose that although some power and authority are inevitable, their radius of action should be minimal" (*CVM II*, 268). "Positive" liberty, by contrast, is "more social than individual since it is based on the very just idea that the possibility that every individual has of deciding his destiny is subsumed to a great extent by 'social' factors beyond his control" (*CVM II*, 269). Paralleling the classical arguments of those who adhere to this notion of freedom, Vargas asks, "how can an illiterate take advantage of a free press? Of what use is the freedom to travel to a person living in poverty? Does the freedom to work mean the same thing to the owner of a business as it does to an unemployed worker?" (*CVM II*, 269). Vargas suggests that inherent in the concept of "negative" freedom is the idea that each individual is essentially unique, while the "positive" concept assumes and stresses the notion that there is "more liberty . . . when there are fewer differences in the social body, when the community is more homogeneous" (*CVM II*, 269). Although he feels that all totalitarian states—whether of the right or the left—tend to give greater weight to this "positive" concept of freedom, it has, nevertheless, led to a multitude of benefits for humanity, not the least of which is the recognition of what has to be called "social consciousness": "the notions of human solidarity, and social responsibility and the idea of justice have been enriched and expanded thanks to the 'positive' concept of liberty. It has also served to counteract or abolish evils such as slavery, racism, . . . and discrimination" (*CVM II*, 270). Following Berlin, Vargas Llosa refuses to consider one of these concepts as false and the other as true; and although he realizes that when followed absolutely one cancels the other, he favors a kind of balance between the two: "in practical terms—in social life, in history—the ideal is to try to achieve a transaction between both concepts. The societies that have been able to bring about a compromise between both forms of freedom are those that have achieved the most worthy and most just levels of life" (*CVM II*, 271). This practical, eclectic, and difficult stance suggests that Vargas's position cannot be conveniently labeled as "conservative" or "neoliberal," as some have attempted to do.[42]

We have already noted Vargas Llosa's frequent and sympathetic comment on the work of Jorge Edwards as well as his praise of Octavio Paz. Scattered throughout his essayistic work one can also find occasional references to other contemporaries whose ideas resonate with his own. Among such writers—authors whom he singles out as having fulfilled their "civic functions" as dissenters—is Gabriel Zaid (*CVM II*, 409ff.). The Mexican essayist, it will be recalled, was trained as an engineer, gained considerable recognition as a poet, and has written a number of highly unorthodox essays, notably those in the collections *El progreso improductivo* and *Como leer en bicicleta*. The latter, incidentally, was very favorably reviewed by Vargas Llosa in the popular Peruvian weekly *Caretas*.[43]

Zaid's views on economics, already discussed in chapter 3 in connection with the question of *desarrollismo*, are decidedly those of a maverick. His espousal of limited "appropriate" technologies for Mexico and the Third World, rather than the grandiose schemes of developmental bureaucrats, is illustrative of his thinking. On a more political level, many might consider his ideas to be essentially neoconservative, if not almost reactionary. Others, noting his frequent attacks on bureaucracy, planners, paternalistic statism, and organized do-gooders, the "lucrative profession of helping the disadvantaged," as he views it, might consider him somewhat of a modern libertarian or simply an old-fashioned nineteenth-century liberal. What is abundantly clear is that in his effort to avoid being labeled he identifies strongly with individualists who are not afraid to champion the public good: not surprisingly, he writes glowingly of Ralph Nader's battles with North American big business and of Andrei Sakarov's defiance of the Soviet scientific establishment (*PI*, 189–190). What he apparently prefers over the usual political categories is a position supporting "the public" (understood as an unorganized agglomeration of individuals) in its struggle against bureaucracies and interest groups, be they governmental, industrial, or whatever (*PI*, 189).

Zaid frequently appears to be a voice crying in a wilderness of contemporary trendiness, impersonality, and hypocrisy. Yet he is hardly a desperate or anguished writer. As we have already seen, his distinctive tone is more often than not that of a humorist. This aspect of his work is especially obvious in *Como leer en bicicleta*, a collection covering more than ten years of contributions to such journals as *Siempre*, *Plural*, *Vuelta*, and others. Here Zaid's targets are the radical chic, or *rábanos* (radishes; i.e., red on the outside, white on the inside), as he calls them, as well as his own kind—the literati and other intellectuals. Such pieces as "To Whom It May Concern," an apocryphal want ad for an ideal literary critic, or "Regarding the Production of Impressive Eulogies," on the need for a computerized program for the efficient production of eulogies (an item evidently in great demand among Mexican intellectuals), illustrate

Zaid's wit at its best. Similarly, his sly critique of a modish Marxism is perhaps best exemplified in a delicious put-down titled, "How Marx Came and Went."[44] Zaid's work after the publication of *Como leer en bicicleta* reveals a similar use of poker-faced humor to jibe the left. A good example appears in the journal *Vuelta* in a very "scientific" study, "Polymetric Letter." In this piece Zaid analyzes apparently real statistics which demonstrate a direct relationship between wealth and districts registering the highest percentage of communist votes: "Mexico is a country where radicalism increases with income . . . To be a leftist and live in the Pedregal, have a house in Cuernavaca, and travel abroad . . . are things that are tolerated."[45]

While Zaid has lent a playful, often ironic note to the polemics surrounding ideology, it is the passionate and articulate voice of Octavio Paz that has dominated the chorus of dissent that has characterized the essay of recent decades. As has been noted, his views have also prompted some of the sharpest reactions among his compatriots.[46] Like so many mature intellectuals of the hemisphere, Paz had early sympathies with leftist ideology, though his position, strongly influenced by the French surrealists, was always somewhat unorthodox.[47] His doubts regarding ideology, especially Marxism, were already evident in his classic work *El laberinto de la soledad*; however, they are further developed in more recent essays such as *Posdata*, *Conjunciones y disjunciones* (Conjunctions and disjunctions, 1969), and *Los hijos del limo*. They become central in *El ogro filantrópico* and *Tiempo nublado*.

We saw that in *Posdata*, while commenting on Tlatelolco, Paz presented a hard-hitting attack on the Mexican political establishment. In the same essay we also noted his doubts regarding the appropriateness of developmental models offered by both the Western capitalistic states and the Soviets. In his discussion of this issue he presents an analysis of revolution illustrative of his pragmatic rather than ideological approach to sociopolitical questions. He offers a broad view based upon his observations of the course of all twentieth-century revolutions:

> There are two kinds of revolutions: those that are the consequence of development (historical, economic, as well as cultural), of which the most perfect example is the French revolution; and those that break out precisely because of insufficient development. I am not even sure if the latter should properly be called revolutions. Whatever they might be called, what is certain is that they are movements which when they are successful must face up to the problem of development, and in order to resolve this problem they sacrifice their other social and political objectives . . . All these revolutions, from the Russian to the Mexican,

... degenerate into bureaucratic regimes that are more or less paternalistic and oppressive. (*P*, 94–95)

This sweeping generalization implies, of course, a clear rejection of such Third World movements as the Cuban revolution, the Marxist program in Central America, and so on. He concludes this part of his discussion by affirming that "any revolution without critical thinking, without the freedom to contradict those in power, and without the possibility of peacefully replacing one rule for another is a revolution that defeats itself. It is a fraud . . . We must renounce definitively the authoritarian tendency of the revolutionary tradition, especially of its Marxist wing" (*P*, 100).

Does Paz suggest then that the Western, free enterprise (specifically North American) model is more appropriate for Mexico and similar nations seeking change? This question cannot be answered easily. Clearly he considers certain characteristics of Western regimes to be highly desirable. For example, paralleling Vargas Llosa's thinking on these issues, he views political democracy and the unconditional exercise of criticism—free speech—as *the* definers of modernity (*P*, 96). However, deep within Paz's thinking there is a powerful current that prevents him from accepting the values of the West and especially of the United States. Since his earliest writings[48] he has cherished a kind of Edenic vision that sees authentic man as existing in a liberated state exempt from toil and wherein his desires—corporeal as well as spiritual—are given free rein in an eternal present. These rather mystical notions, fortified by his readings of the surrealists, Oriental philosophy, and the poetry of Holderlin, Blake, Rilke, and others, hardly constitute an ideology; rather, they serve to undermine existing political or economic ideologies and to make Paz a unique and complex figure among the essayists we have been discussing. In *Posdata* he provides an inkling of how these concepts color his view of the world. For example, in his analysis of the widespread student protests of the late 1960s he states that in addition to various local situations, the underlying cause of this movement was that the students "opposed the implacable phantasm of the future with the spontaneous reality of the now." He goes on to explain,

The eruption of the now signifies, in the very midst of contemporary life, the forbidden word, the cursed word: *pleasure*. A word that is no less explosive nor less beautiful than the word *justice*. When I say pleasure I am not thinking of setting up a new hedonism nor the return to the ancient sensual wisdom—though the former would not be too bad and the latter might even be desirable—but rather I am thinking of the revelation of that dark half of man that has been humiliated and buried by the morality of progress: of that half that is revealed in the images of art and in love. The definition of man as a being that works should be changed for that of a being that desires. (*P*, 27)

It is perhaps unnecessary to note that these are hardly the ideas of a person who would embrace the values and ideology of contemporary North America.

In his later collection, *Los hijos del limo*, the same notions emerge even more clearly. In this very provocative work Paz is primarily concerned with the course of poetry from the romantic revolution to the present. However, and as those familiar with his other writings on the subject might expect, Paz characteristically brings his aesthetic concerns to bear upon practical contemporary problems. Better stated, for a writer of his temperament and beliefs, poetics and politics are by their very nature inseparable. Thus, as we noted in chapter 2, he views the restiveness and rebelliousness of the late 1960s and early 1970s as a reaction against the "Protestant and capitalist ethic with its moral code of savings and work." These recent undercurrents, he feels, "postulate a devaluation of the future" and, most important, "the insurrection of corporeal and orgiastic values is a rebellion against man's twofold penalty—condemnation to work and repression of desire" (*CM*, 156–157). It is a short step from this descriptive statement to a prescription for our times: "the time has come to build an Ethics and Politics upon the Poetics of the now. Politics ceases to be a construction of the future, its mission is to make the present habitable" (*CM*, 157). The fact that Paz declines to explain just how such a politics might come about may disturb some; others could argue that the tone and objective of a work such as *Los hijos del limo* would make the setting forth of any concrete sociopolitical scheme inappropriate.

The entire question of Paz's critique of ideology is intimately connected with his views toward history and his concept of the future. Since modern ideologies have characteristically projected toward the future, their appeal has depended upon our faith that the historical processes of the past and present will continue: in short, that the future will in a real sense be shaped by what has preceded it. Yet Paz, relying heavily on the evidence offered by contemporary art, argues that "now, in the second half of the twentieth century, certain signs indicate a change in our system of beliefs. The conception of history as a progressive and linear process has proved inconsistent." He further argues that "the modern era is beginning to lose faith in itself" (*CM*, 150). Unlike previous centuries, characterized by "naive" applications of strongly historicist progressivism and, of course, Marxism, recent years reveal "a sharp change: people begin to look fearfully toward the future, and what only yesterday seemed the marvels of progress have become its disasters. The future is no longer the storehouse of perfection but of horror" (*CM*, 150). In support of this position he cites the pessimistic views of scientists, demographers, and ecologists. He then turns to a detailed analysis of Marxism, "probably the most coherent and most daring expression of history as a progressive and linear process," in his view. He reminds us that "for Marx history is a single process—the same for all mankind—that unfolds like a mathematical series or a logical proposition. Each proposition generates an opposition resolved in affirmation. In this way, through negations and contradictions, new stages are evolved . . . Each historical period marks an advance on the preceding one, and in each period one social class takes upon itself the representation of all humanity: feudal aristocracy, bourgeoisie, proletariat" (*CM*, 151–152). However, Paz asserts, events of recent years clearly deny the validity of this historical process—truly proletarian revolutionary movements have not taken place, and the revolutions that have triumphed "have been transformed into regimes which are anomalous from a strict Marxist point of view" (*CM*, 152). Although Paz in this context is undeniably thinking of the Soviets, the Chinese, and the Cubans, his objective here is not the criticism of these regimes per se but, rather, the critique of the way people conceive of history. Therefore, he contends that this apparent "aberration" in the development of socialism (i.e., its transformation into dictatorial, bureaucratic states)

> disappears if we give up the conception of history as a progressive, linear process blessed with an imminent rationality. It is hard to resign ourselves to this because giving up this belief implies the end of our claims to shape the future. Nevertheless, it is not a renunciation of socialism as ethical and political *free choice* but of the idea of socialism as a *necessary product* of the historical process. Criticism of the political and moral aberrations of contemporary "socialisms" should begin with criticism of our intellectual aberrations. History is not single . . . it is the history of men and of the marvelous diversity of societies and civilizations which men have created. (*CM*, 153)

In his later collections Paz maintains this critical stance toward ideology; in addition, he becomes more specific in his attacks. His target in these more recent essays are those institutions—especially the state—that have made ideology an instrument of control and self-aggrandizement. The very title of his 1979 collection, *El ogro filantrópico*, is an ambiguous metaphor: the modern state has become "the philanthropic ogre." He offers abundant examples of the ogre's incursions in such places as the Soviet Union, but also in his own Mexico. He is especially vehement in his assault upon state-supported—and thus state-controlled—activity in the arts. Consistent with his underlying critique of ideology, he notes that the incorporation of state-sponsored ideology into the arts results in an emasculated "official art" and the production of mere propaganda. He sees this as having happened in such areas as the celebrated mural painting of postrevolutionary Mexico and in the nation's literature of the same period (*OF*, 7). As in earlier essays he repeatedly stresses the role of untrammeled discussion, of criticism as the only antidote against "the worst of intoxications: ideology" (*OF*, 276). And, like his friend Vargas Llosa (to whom he dedicates a portion of this book), he finds that the universities are failing to meet their obligation of providing a truly open forum. In a long essay, "Terrified Terrorist Doctors," he discusses not only the suppression of students and faculty by the Mexican government but also the de facto censorship imposed by "politically correct" forces within the academic community. As we might expect, it is the Marxists who bear the brunt of his attack. After pointing out that the underlying goal of the 1968 student movement was a general democratization of the nation as well as of educational institutions, he observes: "the left is the natural heir of the 1968 movement but in recent years it has not devoted itself to democratic organization but to the representation . . . of the revolution in university theaters. Perverted by years of Stalinism and afterward influenced by *castrista* and *guevarista caudillismo*, the Mexican left has not been able to recover its original democratic vocation" (*OF*, 157). Contemporary Mexican Marxists, he continues, offer no viable solutions to the nation's problems; they are given to endless rhetoric and, in short, flee from reality. He concludes, "The road to reality is through democratic organization: the public forum, not the cloister or catacomb, these are the places of politics" (*OF*, 157).

Other major themes in *El ogro filantrópico* are the problems of development, North America's relationship toward its southern neighbors (in which he makes clear that his critique of the left should not be taken as support for Yankee racism, imperialism, or atomic policies), and his constant preoccupation with eros and the erotic. Even in the latter area, Paz sees ideology as a destructive force. In a lengthy and fascinating essay, "La mesa y el lecho," he finds—following the unconventional idea of nineteenth-century French visionary Charles Fourier—certain analogies between eros and gastronomy. The details of this curious parallel need not be pursued here, though the repercussions of Paz's observation that the Puritans eschewed spices in their food might well be pondered. At any rate, much of this text revolves about the "decadence of love" in the contemporary world. The modern concept of love, he argues, is different from that of earlier centuries since it has developed within a nonreligious context and "has nourished itself on ideology" (*OF*, 233). He remarks in passing that the sexual revolution ("la rebelión erótica," in his terms) which has flourished in the United States and Northern Europe has incorporated many laudable ethical and social objectives. However, he rejects the politicization of the movement: "it is certain that women have been oppressed in all civilizations, but it is not certain that relations between men and women can be reduced to a relationship of political, economic, or social domination . . . No, the essence of eroticism is not political" (*OF*, 234).[49]

Many of the essays in *Tiempo nublado*, the last of Paz's works to be considered here, are focused on specific events and situations—the Palestinian-Israeli question, communist repression in Poland, the problems of ethnic autonomy within the Soviet Union, and the continuing totalitarian drift of the Cuban state. His treatment of these issues demonstrates clearly that he prefers practical solutions over those derived from ideological abstractions. Thus, in *Tiempo nublado* he welcomes such heterodox movements as Eurocommunism and the then new Spanish social democrats: "the pragmatism of democratic parties, especially of the social democrats, has positive aspects."[50] He seems especially pleased that these groups have abandoned revolutionary praxis and rhetoric: "to renounce revolutionary verbalism is not only a sign of intellectual sobriety but also of political probity" (*TN*, 27). In broadest terms, Paz's devotion to democracy and to its emphasis on free speech and open criticism dominates his thinking. He has even stated that the economic, material achievements of modern industrial societies are intimately related to Western democracy: "democracy has made possible struggle and negotiation between capitalists and workers . . . Productive capacity, the freedom to organize, the right to strike, the ability to bargain: this is what has made the democracies of the West viable and prosperous" (*TN*, 25). He does, however, recognize some of the shortcomings and internal conflicts of the Western democracies. He is particularly critical of their worship of the status quo, of their limited historical vision, and, with regard to the United States, of this country's lack of direction, lack of a sense of project: "what lies behind this richness? I can't answer: I find nothing . . . all of North America's institutions, its technology, its science, its energy, its education are a means, a *toward* something . . . everything is an instrument for . . . what? Ultimate ends, those that really count because they give meaning to our lives, do not appear on the horizon of the United States" (*TN*, 36–37). Paz is especially critical of North America's other deep "contradiction"; namely, its devotion to democracy at home while it pursues imperialist policies abroad (*TN*, 39). Yet despite these reservations, on balance the pragmatic, contradictory West wins easily over the bureaucratized, ideologically dominated Marxist nations. In sum, "the contradictions with totalitarian 'socialism' are more profound and irreconcilable than those of capitalist democracies" (*TN*, 157).

We may close on a prophetic note. The final text of *Tiempo nublado* deals specifically with unrest in the Eastern bloc. Paz, writing, it must be remembered, in the early 1980s, observes: "the cycle of rebellion in the Russian empire has not been closed. The workers movement crushed in 1981 has only been a chapter—though an important one—in the history of the people's struggle against bureaucratic domination: [of] Poles, Czechs, Hungarians, Rumanians, Bulgarians, Cubans, Vietnamese, Cambodians, Afghans, and the various nations within the Empire: Ukrainians, Lithuanians, Tartars, and so many others, without forgetting the Russians themselves . . . The list is long, as is history: it is as long as time itself" (*TN*, 209).

Toward a New Essay

In the previous chapter I cited Julio Cortázar's provocative statement regarding the need for more "Che Guevaras of language, revolutionaries of literature, rather than literati of revolution." I suggested that Cortázar apparently believed that the writing of innovative, often disturbing literature would in some way further the cause of revolutionary change. It would be difficult, if not impossible, to prove or disprove this notion, and it would not be easy to find other writers who have expressed the same idea in such unequivocal terms. Yet one suspects that many other essayists of the period have sensed that their commitment to literature included the obligation to awaken, to stimulate, and to jar their readers into new ways of looking at the world and its problems. To accomplish these objectives, they felt, formal innovations could be as effective as content itself. This attitude explains in part the rich stylistic, structural, and linguistic pyrotechnics found in a closely related genre of the period, Latin America's celebrated "new narrative." In even broader terms, it may also lie behind the experiments and transgressions of that ill-defined international movement—or sensibility—that we have come to call postmodernism.

The relationship of the highly acclaimed *nueva narrativa* to the Spanish American essay of recent decades is not difficult to establish. In general terms, the remarkable success, the "boom," of the hemisphere's prose fiction during the 1960s no doubt encouraged all writers to abandon traditional presentation and to experiment. In several cases (Cortázar, Vargas Llosa, Fuentes, and Cabrera Infante being the most obvious), the new novelists also wrote essays. In other cases, the mood, techniques, and texture of the *nueva narrativa* are clearly reflected in essayistic work. A good example of this phenomenon may be seen in Carlos Monsiváis's *Amor perdido*, in which the work's multiple authorial voices, "show business" format, and other stylistic details resemble, to a considerable degree, a novel such as Cabrera Infante's *Tres tristes tigres*. I would not propose, however, that all or even most of the essayists of the period under consideration show characteristics typical of the new narrative; yet some similarity between this movement and the recent essay seems undeniable. Specifically, this parallelism is supported by such features as (1) richness and variety of authorial voices, (2) frequent and playful use of foreign words or phrases, (3) other linguistic gambits such as extreme irony or using the taboo lexicon of sex and the erotic, (4) the use of novel framing devices or unusual formats, (5) a marked penchant for humor, an element not especially strong in the essay—or novel—of earlier years, and, (6) a strong sense of authorial self-consciousness.

In addition to these similarities to the *nueva narrativa* other unusual elements may be found in the new essay.[1] Though "poetic prose" may not be new or very accurately defined, this quality or tonality does dominate a number of recent essays. Such works as Octavio Paz's *El mono gramático* (*The Monkey Grammarian*, 1974) or Julio Cortázar's *Prosa del observatorio* (Prose from the observatory, 1972) illustrate this phenomenon particularly well. Another interesting formal feature of many recent essays involves the mixing of genres. The entire question of genre boundaries, of what constitutes a "pure" as opposed to a "hybrid" literary form, has fascinated and vexed critics for many years; however, I do not wish to become involved in the technical discussion surrounding this issue. It is sufficient to take note of certain unclassifiable texts wherein expository, "essayistic" elements blend, at times quite happily, with narrative material; or of other works where an entirely nonliterary format—such as a technical-sounding business report—may be ironically used to present an essayist's views. Why genre mixing of this kind should be employed during a particular period or in a particular place is another intriguing matter. A number of commentators—German critic Theodor Adorno has been one of the most articulate in this regard[2]—have suggested that in authoritarian regimes there is little tolerance for aesthetic (in this case, literary) hybridization; thus those who violate generic boundaries may in some way be perceived as threatening the established order, as being genuine aesthetic troublemakers. While no actual examples of an essayist being prosecuted by the authorities specifically for the heinous crime of having produced a literary hybrid can be offered, this view of genre mixing does support my contention that not only in terms of content but also by virtue of its formal innovations the new essay has been a vehicle of dissent.

THE AUTONOMOUS TEXT

One of the most fascinating aspects of the "new essay" may be seen in certain practices based on attitudes regarding the autonomy of language, the self-referential nature of text, and even the notion of the book as artifact, as an entity possessing a kind of life of its own beyond, or in addition to, its semiotic function. Several of the new novelists also viewed language and the printed page in the same manner, so it should not surprise us that one of these, Cortázar, in his essayistic work, should reveal this sensibility. Note, for example, his playful mini-essay, "Pida la palabra, pero tenga cuidado" (Ask to speak, but be careful) in *Ultimo round*: "when Herr Professor Dr. Lastra took the words out of my mouth, they bit him fiercely, leaving his hand a bloody mess. Like so many others Dr. Lastra didn't know that when you take hold of a word you have to be damn sure of grabbing it by the fur of the neck, if, for example, it's the word *ola* [wave], but *queja* [complaint] you have to hold by its paws, while *asa* [handle, grip] requires you to delicately slip your fingers beneath it as when one waves a piece of toast around before spreading it with butter" (*UR*, pb, 96). The same collage collection, *Ultimo round*, also illustrates Cortázar's fascination with the book as object, as an artifact/symbol whose total design carries a semiotic charge greater than the sum of its parts. Thus, in addition to its unique covers (mock-ups of the front page of a newspaper), the original single-volume edition startled readers (and confounded scholars faced with a difficult problem in noting pagination) by its "two-story" format—independent split pages providing a larger "main floor" for some two-thirds of the material and a *planta baja*, or ground-floor "bargain basement," for the remainder. One wonders if there is any thematic connection between the same page of the two "floors" or if it is essentially just another means to encourage reader participation.[3] Indeed, a cynical observer might well say that it is simply a cheap trick to attract attention. Though the real structure of *Ultimo round* may not be found in its unique pagination (in fact, in more recent paperback editions it has been supplanted by two conventional volumes), the book is unified in another way. The first prose selection, "Descripción de un combate o a buen entendedor" (Description of a fight or to those who understand), and the very last piece, "A los malos entendedores" (To those who don't understand), provide a framing device which suggests that the apparent miscellany in fact consists of several loosely related themes orchestrated by differing textual techniques. As Calac, the folksy *porteño* interlocutor of the two pieces, puts it, "Don't forget, the same thing can be shown in fifty different ways" (*UR*, 217).

In some respects *La vuelta al día en ochenta mundos* is a similar literary production. Like *Ultimo round* it is a handsome book that features an eye-catching cover illustration (a kind of "animated" series of drawings depicting boys playing leap-frog who are gradually transformed into real frogs), an endpaper design composed of miscellaneous things (bottles, horses, binoculars, boots, dogs, chickens, hats, etc.), and a rich variety of illustrations throughout. In titling this work Cortázar takes his cue from "another Julio": somewhat like Verne's characters who travel round the world in a fixed period, in *Vuelta al día* the author travels through his very personal inner universe, what he calls "the sponge through which fish of memory continually enter and leave, exploding alliances of times, states, and materials that seriousness, that lady too frequently heeded, would consider to be irreconcilable."[4] Cortázar's work, however, really bears little resemblance to its French predecessor; rather, it is the spirit of Verne's venture—a madcap race round the world contrasting sharply with the stolid, practical ambience of late nineteenth-century Europe—which provides a tenuous link between the two authors.

In *Vuelta al día* Cortázar provides rich evidence of his unorthodox attitudes toward language. Like other new essayists (Octavio Paz, for example), he was intrigued by analogies; not mere metaphors, but entire systems of analogous relationships. That words might be thought of as functioning parts of a machine or that a machine could be seen as a discursive organization seems to have been one of the key ideas in his mind when he wrote "De otra máquina célibe" (Regarding another celibate [a pun on 'celebrated'] machine). Note in this regard his epigraph for the essay, taken from a Michel Foucault text on surrealist precursor Raymond Roussel: "manufactured from language, machines are that very fabrication in action; they are their own birth repeated in themselves; among their tubes, their gears, their metallic connections" (*VDM*, I, 121). The machine that Cortázar then proceeds solemnly to describe in his essay is the celebrated "Rayuela-matic," an automatic device for deciphering the complexities of his novel *Rayuela*. Given the analogic relationship of texts and machines it is a short step from a well-functioning piece of verbal apparatus to considering a verbal organism consisting of parts terribly misassembled. This notion may help explain another of the short experimental texts in *Vuelta al día*: "Dos historietas zoológicas y otra casi" (Two zoological tales and almost another). In this partly narrative, partly expository piece, one paragraph is purportedly composed by a chicken: "with that which happens is us carry away. Quickly of the possessed world we are hurray. It was an offensive apparently launched Canaveral Americans Cape by the from" (VDM, I, 170).[5] The entire text must be read in the original to savor its supreme verbal madness or to produce an acceptable translation. While the piece says something about the supposed effect of a misfired rocket on a community of chickens, the "content" is clearly of little moment. As in many texts of recent decades, the medium is the message. The disjointed syntax of the piece and its accompanying graphic enhancement—a completely unsettling drawing of a four-footed bowlegged hen—may simply strike us as more or less funny, though I suspect Cortázar is also telling us something about the arbitrary nature of syntax and, of course, something about the forbidden joys of sheer verbal idiocy. Cortázar is an especially rich source of material illustrative of linguistic gamesmanship, of language-as-an-object, of words as self-referential "empty" signifiers, and of the sensitivity toward the physical aspect of the literary artifact. We shall return to him elsewhere in this chapter, but for the moment other practitioners of this art will be considered.

The interest in total book design, for example, is seen also in the work of such recent essayists as Guillermo Cabrera Infante (1929–   ), Zaid, Monsiváis, and the talented but relatively unknown Guatemalan, Augusto Monterroso (1921–   ). Monsiváis's *Amor perdido*, a good illustration of this concern, features in its front material an index or table of contents which resembles a theatrical playbill more than anything else. Its well-chosen photographs are placed in the middle of the book and are presented on substantial cardboard with a blank postal card design on the reverse of each. A reader might, if he or she wished, remove the photos and mail them—a small bonus for the volume's purchaser. On the back cover is the author's own text describing the book in the tone of a nightclub master of ceremonies: "esteemed audience, with you tonight, direct from their triumphant tour . . ." Monterroso, whom we shall later consider in connection with his experiments in genre mixing, has also produced, in collaboration with a graphic artist, Vicente Rojo, a remarkable example of total book design, the essayistic potpourri *La palabra mágica* (The magic word, 1983). Amply and often ironically illustrated, this slender volume features multicolor type, appropriate reprints of old engravings, whimsical original line drawings by the author, arbitrarily positioned numbers indicating pagination, and, in general terms, a decidedly ludic spirit. Furthermore, the subject of several of the texts deals with literary experimentation and novel ideas regarding genre—the obituary as a literary form, for example. Monterroso, who has stated, "regarding erudition, what attracts me most is the game," underscores his playful attitude toward literary artifice by frequent references to such soulmates as the Baroque masters Quevedo and Góngora as well as Jorge Luis Borges.[6] But one is struck even more by his unstated affinity to Cortázar, especially with regard to matters of book design and format. Like the Argentine's *Ultimo round* or *La vuelta al día en ochenta mundos*, Monterroso's *La palabra mágica* bears a semiotic charge that translates as an invitation for the reader to handle, peruse, and play with the book as with a toy. Curiously, direct mention of

Cortázar is infrequent in Monterroso's work, though the Guatemalan essayist has obviously been a devout admirer of the Argentinean.[7] Cuba's Guillermo Cabrera Infante is usually considered a writer of narrative fiction rather than an essayist. Although he was born in Latin America like Cortázar, Cabrera has spent a good deal of his adult life abroad—in his case, in England. Of course the parallel would not include political orientation since the Cuban has been an outspoken critic of Castro and his regime's Marxist orientation, while Cortázar's strong leftist sympathies have already been noted. As essayists, however, they have much in common: both are verbal experimenters who obviously enjoy shocking their readers with linguistic acrobatics. The two also share a fascination with the literary artifact: the unnerving title, the offbeat book jacket, collage, and the unusually formated printed page. It is true that Cabrera has been less prolific than Cortázar and few would consider him as talented a writer as the Argentinean, yet his work as an essayist is substantial and illustrates nicely the wide diffusion of what I have termed the "new essay."

Readers who are familiar with Cabrera's most celebrated work, the novel *Tres tristes tigres*, where rich wordplay may be found on almost every page, will not be overly surprised by his essays. His two collections in the genre (if this term can be applied to these monuments to generic chaos) are interestingly titled *O* (1975) and *Exorcismos de esti(l)o* (Exorcisms of style, 1976). The first title invites speculation. What is the significance of the letter *O*, a perfect circle celebrated by Pythagoreans and mystics, and perhaps an echo of a classical work of French eroticism, Pauline Reage's *The Story of O*?[8] The second title presents a minor problem in the not terribly clever bracketing within the word *estilo* (style), which without the *l* becomes *estío*, a poetic term for "summer." Despite its unusual title, the first collection is somewhat more traditional than *Exorcismos*. Eroticism and the related themes of pornography and censorship are woven into about half of the texts, supporting to some extent the relationship to Reage and French erotic writing. The volume is framed by opening and closing pieces describing "swinging London" of the 1960s. Both of these texts are laden with pop references, show biz glitz, ample samples of bilingual (chiefly English/Spanish) puns, wordplay, and other rather self-conscious linguistic games. "Swinging London," for example, appears as "Lwinging Sondon," "Swyngyng Lyndyn," and so on. The English word "wow!" complete with exclamation point, is interjected at appropriate (?) times. Epigraphs, quotations, intertextual echoes, and long enumerations of then popular figures (Mary Quant, The Beatles, Twiggy, Englebert Humperdinck) spice—or perhaps dilute—the text. The pieces are in effect essays in pop culture as well as essays on pop culture. The medium is the message, or at least part of the message. Yet several of the items in *O* are true essays having substantive content. The two pieces on pornography, "An Innocent Pornography" and "Another Innocent Pornographer," are genuine attempts at defining this literary phenomenon. "Careful, don't touch," a wry comment on the familiar pop-culture ritual of the beauty contest, is enriched by several fine divagations dealing with such varied matters as the medieval cult of woman, the foibles of international beauty-pageant politics (can Miss Gibraltar and Miss Spain be on the same platform?), and the British penchant for wagering on everything. One of the longest essays, "Forms of Folk Poetry," gives Cabrera the opportunity to cite a wide variety of Spanish and English song lyrics and folk poetry. His quotation of limericks in both languages is especially outrageous and leads us to believe that the primary objective of this essay is simply to showcase such juicy tidbits as the following:

> Un político de apellido Castro
> quiso ser del marxismo un astro.
>   Y aunque lo quiso mucho, mucho,
>   Como Marx no llegó ni a Groucho
> Y acabó siendo un politicastro.
> (A *político* by the name of Castro
> Wanted to be a Marxist astro
>   Though he wanted this very mucho
>   As a Marx he wasn't even a Groucho
> He wound up by being merely a *politicastro*.)[9]

Cabrera concludes *O* by another reference to his favorite Marx (Groucho, of course, not Karl): "and with this thought, I take leave, dear reader; but I will soon return. However, as Marx says, if you haven't received a letter from me, perhaps it's because I haven't written any."[10]

Exorcismos de esti(l)o, as its title suggests, is almost a pure exercise in stylistics, if not typography. In it Cabrera *says* very little, though he *does* a great deal. The first page is a "Dédicace [sic]" to "happy, varied, diverse commas": the pages following consist of various brief momentous thoughts on literature of which the following is a good example: "*Literatura* is *littérature* in French, and *litter* is 'trash,' 'refuse' in English; while *rature*, again in French, is 'erasure,' and *lit* is 'bed'—that bed where I lie down to produce literature: only in Spanish *literatura* doesn't mean anything else."[11] It would be difficult and perhaps tedious to attempt extensive citation from *Exorcismos*, especially because most of its pages must be seen to be appreciated. For example, one rambling piece has no written punctuation but registers periods, commas, question marks, and functions of a typewriter (space bar, carriage) by spelling them out in the text.

The self-conscious author seems to be someone playing with a typewriter or perhaps is the machine itself:

> To speak of Narcissus erasure parenthesis but comma question mark
> not everyone will speak hyphen close parenthesis and of the stream as
> the first mirror that on waking Narcissus nervous becomes the first
> neither lucid nor obscure camera but rather an unstable one period . . .
> It is possible to speak of the mirror image without speaking of
> Narcissus also so so to speak eak eak d d d Echo Echo Echo period
> What wisdom the Ancient Greeks had when they related the image in
> water slash hyphen mirror slash with the sound image of the echo and
> join Narcissus and Echo as lovers condemned to be reflections comma
> . . . (*EE*, 22)

In other texts of the collection he discusses puns (and puns while doing so), produces a series of taboo words by the deliberate use of endline hyphens (*dis-putas, cená-culos, ano-tador*), punningly provides a series of "daffynitions" (*vo-caburlarios*), and presents a number of short texts followed by half-serious exercises or questions-for-the-student in the manner of a pedagogic workbook. Like a tireless stand-up comedian Cabrera often gets a good laugh, but his obsessive quest for applause frequently misfires. One of the collection's longer essays (most of the book's texts barely fill half a page), "Obras maestras desconocidas," illustrates this failing rather well. Subtitled "El concerto para el pie izquierdo de Morritz Ravelli" (Concerto for the left foot by Morritz Ravelli), the piece is a madhouse of garbled historical information, wordplay based on famous proper names, and multilingual puns. Maurice Ravel is presented as the "famous Albanian composer" Morritz Ravelli; a celebrated physician and musicologist appears as Dr. Schweitzer-Lagerbeer; apocryphal bibliographic references are thrown in along with footnotes telling us about the assassination of the "Grand Prix Sarajebo or Sarah-Jebó," an act that "started the Boxer War"; and at the essay's conclusion he promises another piece on "La música del agua de Gregorio Seltzer" (Gregorio Seltzer's water music)—not especially clever material for the author of the frequently brilliant *Tres tristes tigres*.

THE AUTHOR'S VOICE

One of Cabrera's more effective humorous strategies—though one that he employs sparingly—involves the ironic manipulation of authorial voice. As we shall see, he is not alone among the new essayists who have availed themselves of this time-honored technique. A good example of its use by Cabrera is the whimsical "Peligro de colisión de los museos" (The danger of museum collisions). Feigning solemn journalistic responsibility, he observes, "We have emphasized at great length in our informative columns—always in the service of the nation's general interest—the growing danger of museum collisions" (*EE*, 148). He continues, in the balance of the piece, to describe in the same general tone the dangers of this absurdly impossible happening.

Others, however, have done much more with the effective manipulation of authorial voice. Among the essayists we have been considering, here again Cortázar stands out as a master strategist. Although he often wrote fairly traditional expository prose, much of Cortázar's essayistic work is marked by an unusually strong authorial presence, by many colloquial, ideolectical, personal terms, and by "winks" to those readers who, if sufficiently initiated, become his "accomplices" in the literary game. One of his most telling stratagems is what may be called his "mock serious" voice: using either the first or third person he affects an exaggeratedly serious "establishment" tone for ironic effect. Finally, he often avails himself of the highly experimental "Cronopian" voice:[12] typically first person, highly innovative, decidedly zany, full of literary gamesmanship, and often complemented by graphic enhancements. As might be expected, the unusual nature of these texts can easily create problems for readers not on Cortázar's wavelength.

One of the earliest essays to show his penchant for stylistic novelty and to signal the genesis of his unique authorial voice is "Louis enormísimo cronopio" (Louis, the greatest *cronopio*).[13] This piece is also important for other reasons: it suggests that Cortázar was developing a new relationship to his readers and it marks the debut of his celebrated *cronopios* and *famas* some ten years before they appeared in the volume *Historias de cronopios y famas* (*Cronopios and Famas*, 1962). From the outset the essay—an impressionistic review of a concert Louis Armstrong gave in Paris—is playful, personal, and extremely graphic. The first few lines set the tone:

> It seems that the big boss man, better known as God, blew into the body of the first man to bring him to life and give him a soul. If instead of the boss man Louis had been there to blow, man would have turned out much better. Chronology, history, and other circumstances are a long series of misfortunes. A world begun by a Picasso, instead of ending up with him, would be a world exclusively for *cronopios*; and on every streetcorner *cronopios* would dance the *tregua* and the *catala*; and coming up to the streetlight Louis would blow for hours making big

globs of celestial raspberry syrup fall from the sky for the kids and dogs to gobble up. (*VDM*, II, 13)

Cortázar then sketches the atmosphere of the concert hall and his own ecstatic reactions to the music and even a wild imagined scene on board Armstrong's flight to Paris. The linkage created with his reader is typically Cortazarian in that the sharing of certain knowledge or experiences seems to be assumed by the author: but the reader who has not heard "When It's Sleepy Time Down South," "Confessin," and "Muskrat Ramble" or has never experienced a Trummy Young trombone solo just does not belong to the club— he or she is not a genuine *lector cómplice* and might just as well join the other *famas* who go home to listen to "recommended music."

Cortázar's essayistic work is especially rich in this kind of intimate, chatty writing in which he intertwines personal experiences, nostalgia, and often a confessional note. Some other good examples would be "On the Sense of not Being Completely There," "The Noble Art," "The Sense of the Fantastic" (all in *Vuelta al día*), or one of the essayistic fragments from the more recent *Un tal Lucas* (*A Certain Lucas*, 1984). More often than not pieces of this type also set forth a strong viewpoint or opinion. In "On the Sense of not Being Completely There," for example, he begins by admitting that he loves word games and that he considers himself to be "un niño hombre" (a child-man). He then shows how this general feeling of childlike wonderment has shaped his theory of literary art. Thus, at the essay's conclusion, he presents an ingeniously wrought defense of the ludic elements in *Rayuela* (*VDM*, II, 213).

In a number of the essays cast in this authorial tone, Cortázar makes good use of narrative elements, especially jokes and anecdotes. His delightful plea for more humor in Hispanic letters, "Of Seriousness at Wakes," is a case in point (*VDM*, I, 39–42). In a similar though much shorter piece, "Lucas, His Ecological Meditations," he argues for the joys of urbane, cultivated living as opposed to the voguish enthusiasm for raw nature.[14] In several other of the "Lucas" essays, the chatty first-person voice is used to express the author's opinion on a wide variety of matters. In "What Is a Polygraph," for example, his fondness for highly versatile writers forms the basis for a lively discussion of Samuel Johnson. This piece is especially revealing since Cortázar concludes by explaining—in a half-joking, conversational tone—his concept of books such as his own *Un tal Lucas*:

I have great sympathy for polygraphs who cast their fishing rod everywhere, all the while making believe that they are half asleep like Dr. Johnson, and who figure out how to do exhaustive work on such themes as tea, how to improve the bad taste of milk, the court of Augustus, not to mention Scottish bishops. After all, that's what I'm doing in this book. (*UTL*, 102)

A number of Cortázar's most delightful—and most humorous—texts are the product of his ironic "mock serious" voice. We have already noted the content of one of the best of these, "The Treasure of Youth," in connection with the theme of progress and development discussed in chapter 3. As will be recalled, in this text Cortázar writes in the voice of the establishment, the solid citizen or paterfamilias sermonizing on the subject of youth's lack of appreciation for the marvels of modern technology. The authorial voice exudes middle-class smugness and at times the slick banalities of advertising: parents are "loving parents," the course of science is "a ceaseless search," and the latest invention is "the final link in the chain of progress." This deliberate use of clichés will elicit a smile from many readers and very likely hearty laughter from others.

This same tongue-in-cheek seriousness—what might be called the feigned *fama* voice, to use Cortazarian terms—appears in many other pieces. The completely zany "On the Extermination of Crocodiles in the Auvergne" presents an interesting variation within the mode. Here the authorial voice is that of a bureaucrat making a report, or possibly a rather pompous journalist. The relationship of theme to style is typical of this group of writings: a very proper, very traditional, authoritative third-person voice is used to present outrageously surreal content. In this case the matter under discussion is the well-organized campaign to identify, localize, root out, and eradicate crocodiles in the Auvergne district of France—a project made especially difficult by the minor problem that no one has ever reported the existence of these creatures in the area. This situation does not, however, deter the sophisticated practitioners of applied social science who continue to gather their important data:

> The most sophisticated surveys, based on procedures recommended by the Butantán Institute and the FAO, such as parallel investigations in which the central theme is never questioned but rather peripheral data capable of elucidating by a strictly structural methodology the complete body of desired evidence, have always resulted in complete failure. The police force as well as psychologists charged with these different investigations are convinced that the negative replies and even the stupefaction that is revealed by those questioned prove unequivocally the existence of enormous numbers of crocodiles in the Auvergne. (*UR*, 196)

Despite the apparent total absence of crocodiles, the undaunted authorities prepare vast plans for elimination of the danger, all of which is described in exquisite officialese by the narrator:

> for years the authorities have been preparing the necessary mechanisms for the extermination of the enormous quantities of crocodiles that infest the Auvergne region. Thanks to the enlightened cooperation of UNESCO, the most distinguished African, Indian, and Thai specialists have shared their expertise and have provided instructions that should lead to the elimination of the plague in a few months. In every district center there is an official who enjoys full authority to carry out this tremendous operation against crocodiles. (*UR*, 196)

Other variations of this authorial voice may be found in the "Instruction Manual" section of *Historias de famas y cronopios* and especially in *Un tal Lucas*. "Texturologías" (Texturologies), an example from the latter collection, is little more than a brief literary joke in which several voices emerge in a series of "scholarly" quotations. Somewhat in the spirit of Borges (as in his "Pierre Menard"), Cortázar lampoons overly serious critics by inventing a sequence of quotations attributed to apocryphal, but vaguely believable, publications: *The Phenomenological Review* of Nebraska, the *Sovietskya Biéli* of Mongolia, and *Quel Sel* (!) of Paris. Each citation reflects the tone of the journal and the local slant of the author; moreover, each comes as a response to the preceding critical statement. This chain reaction of solemn literary nonsense is set into motion by the publication of a group of poems by an obscure Bolivian. While "Texturologías" has a slight narrative element, it can certainly be viewed as an essay on the pretensions and gratuitousness of literary—especially academic—criticism. The final citation of the piece is deliberately expressed in the highly charged jargon of the then currently faddish scholarship. Note that in the following a Spanish American is praising a Frenchman's interpretation of the poems in question: "an admirable piece of heuristic work by that Gerard Depardiable . . . one that we might well classify as structurological by dint of its dual ursemiotic richness and its conjoined rigor in an area so given to the merely epiphonemic. I shall leave it to a poet to sum up in a premonitory manner these texturological conquests that clearly foreshadow the parametainfracriticism of the future" (*UTL*, 98).

The Mexican essayists have also produced many texts rich in ironic humor. The late Jorge Ibargüengoitia, for example, may be approached as a skillful and humorous manipulator of authorial voice, despite the fact that his substratum of humor reinforces the very serious concerns of much of his writing.[15]

His light, whimsical touch is best seen in *Viajes en la América ignota* (Travels in undiscovered America, 1972), a collection of essays, costumbristic pieces, and anecdotal travel impressions most of which originally appeared in the newspaper *Excelsior*. Ibargüengoitia's humor relies on a nice mix of understatement, irony, and sly comment regarding everything from the Cuban revolution to his fondness for loafing on the beach. In one section of the *Viajes*, "New Careers," he suggests several important new professions for the developing nation—"applied mythologist," "garbage engineer," and so on.[16] In another, he presents a series of *homenajes* to various institutions and public servants: in his tribute to the police, for example, he notes that they are often so devoted to duty that they will remain on guard absolutely motionless even while a store is being robbed or a woman assaulted. The collection includes barbed comment on social castes in Castro's Cuba, observations on the California life-style, and a look at the North American counterculture movement. But his sharpest attacks are directed toward the tired mythology of the Mexican revolution. In this respect his position frequently parallels that of such diverse writers as Zaid, Monsiváis, or even Cosío Villegas. Thus, his essay on Franco's preparation of Prince Juan Carlos for the Spanish throne provides a nice point of departure for a spoof of Mexico's sexennial political ritual: he suggests that it would not be a bad idea for Mexico to institute a monarchy, for then "coronations would be held in Teotihuacán with dance numbers by the Ballet Folklórico. If human sacrifice would be added, the success would be complete." He notes that this would even attract more tourism, and just to dispel any doubts about his message, he slyly adds that "the coronation would be held every six years" (*V*, 193). Perhaps the best example of Ibargüengoitia's gift for the ironic manipulation of authorial voice is seen in this collection's final text, "A Story for the Revolutionary Child." Briefly, the point of this essay, cast as a "lesson" to a child, is that the egalitarian, nationalistic rhetoric of the revolution represents little more than solemn hypocrisy. "Everything that we see about us, child of the revolution, is a product of the Mexican revolution, which, as we all know, began as an armed movement and was later transformed into a social movement in which all Mexicans, without regard to their class, participate." The narrative voice continues (apparently we are in a supermarket): "over there you can see our richest millionaires pushing shopping carts, just like the poorest folks, putting into them . . . red wine imported from France, smoked salmon from the North Sea . . . caviar from the Black Sea . . . you pay at the checkstand." Shifting perspective, the narrator points out the surprising number of business houses with foreign names: "they are also products of the revolution, because before that event took place, all the capital of Mexico . . . was . . . can you believe it, child of the revolution, in the hands of foreigners!" (*V*, 216–218). Despite the narrative elements, and typical of this groups' innovations, Ibargüengoitia's ironic "lesson" comes across clearly as a genuine essay directed toward a serious end.

Additional examples illustrating the skillful manipulation of authorial voice are not difficult to find among other Mexican essayists. Monsiváis, in both his *Días de guardar* and *Amor perdido*, employs a rich variety of voices to achieve his objectives: like Cabrera Infante, Cortázar, and his compatriot Ibargüengoitia, he is especially effective in his ironic use of the voice of the establishment (*DG*, 65ff.), in his intercalating voices of the lowest socioeconomic groups into high-culture discourse (*AP*, 319–346), and in his technique of blending the slangy, generationally specific voice of youth into more normal literary language (*AP*, 227–262). Gabriel Zaid, another of the Mexican group, demonstrates an equally diverse range of authorial voices. In his *Como leer en bicicleta* we find him appropriating the tone of a stereotypical organization man presenting a technical planning document to his big business colleagues (*CLB*, 22–26), of a newspaper copy editor preparing a want-ad (*CLB*, 57–58), and of a surprisingly entrepreneurial Karl Marx writing letters in an effort to promote his most recent book, *Das Kapital* (*CLB*, 156–162).

GENRE MIXING

When writers like Zaid or Cortázar use a distinctive voice to produce a desired essayistic effect they frequently incorporate into the text additional features associated with other genres and even with nonliterary discourse. Thus, Zaid's piece on Marx noted above is actually presented as a series of letters—in effect, an epistolary essay. Other unusual formats include the technical report (Zaid again), slightly modified newspaper reportage, often featuring interviews (Monsiváis), collage (Cortázar), narrative intercalations (Cortázar and others), and, for want of a better term, the essayistic prose poem (Paz, Cortázar). An examination of some illustrative texts will show how such generic hybrids may, despite their unusual nature, still be considered essays.

Julio Cortázar's "Noticias del mes de mayo," one of the most interesting pieces in *Ultimo round*, is a striking example of how far an essayist can go and still remain faithful to the basic character of the genre. The text itself does not look anything like an essay, and it does not resemble a short story, an article, a poem, or any other familiar literary form. Its many different type fonts (italic, caps, boldface), photos, diagrams, along with other visual enhancements, and formatting into verselike lines interspersed by blocks of prose all support

Cortázar's own characterization of the text as a "collage of memories." Inspired by the activities of French students during the May 1968 uprisings, "Noticias" represents more than a political protest; rather, it is an invitation to join the aroused young rebels in their campaign to invert the established order (in the aesthetic, social, and spiritual sense as well as the political): to become a part of the struggle against *la Gran Costumbre* (the tried and true) or the "Great Stuffy Moth," as Cortázar puts it. In terms of the distinction developed by Octavio Paz and discussed in chapter 2, its basic message is clearly one of rebellion rather than revolution. What concerns us here, however, is the manner in which this highly charged message is transmitted.

Following his opening statement, Cortázar presents in boldface several of the many slogans/graffiti that appeared on the walls of public buildings and are scattered throughout his text: "El sueño es realidad" (Dreaming is reality), "Exagerar es ya un comienzo de invención" (To exaggerate is a beginning of invention). These are followed by more verselike lines describing the birth of what Cortázar has often described poetically as the new "sponge time" or the "porous epoch."[17] These ruminations are interrupted by a bit of enigmatic prose, within parentheses, on the far right of the page: "STOP THE PRESS: [in English] the Mona Lisa expired last night at 8:25 P.M., the victim of indigestion resulting from prefabricated musings. A drop in the price of American Express, Cook, and Exprinter stocks is expected" (*UR*, 48). At the same time he inserts a typical colophon mentioning details of copyright and number of volumes printed. More descriptive lines (prose or verse?) follow; then a double-page photo of posters placed on the walls of an academic hall and several more student slogans copied from the graffiti on various buildings: "Unbutton your brain as frequently as you unbutton your fly," "Orthography is a bureaucrat," and so on. Cortázar then goes on to cite a student manifesto and Jean-Paul Sartre's comment on the existential nature of the Cuban revolution: "what is admirable in the case of Castro is that theory was born of experience rather than preceding it" (*UR*, 50). Further textual material is punctuated by photos of posters and by such delicious slogans as "Be realists: ask for the impossible," "The revolution is unbelievable because it is true," or "We are calm: two plus two is no longer four."[18] Also included at strategic points in the essay are quotations from such figures as philosopher Herbert Marcuse, radical leader Rudi Dutschke, and student activist Daniel Cohn-Bendit. Random thoughts crop up within parentheses or are placed boldface throughout the text. Note a typical ironically charged example cited in French: "On est poli, on est discret, on est français, on est terriblement intélligent" (*UR*, 59). Occasionally Cortázar attempts to make a point by means of a diagram, designed no doubt to tweak the establishment and perhaps scholars fond of diagrammatic explanations. Thus he again describes *la Gran Costumbre* as

$$\text{System} \overset{\displaystyle \text{Liberty}}{\underset{\displaystyle \text{Equality}}{\text{— Fraternity —}}} \text{My Ass}$$

(UR, 57)

One of the most interesting—and effective—features of "Noticias del mes de mayo" is the abrupt but strategic insertion of what would appear to be an overheard voice or private conversation:

> Well then, poetry . . . / Poetry? Oh dear me, no / What a shame, to think that it was doing so well until just a few years ago, despite certain verbal excess, and now, suddenly . . . / It must be Moscow's money, if it's not dollars from the CIA, which also paid Cohn-Bendit / to insult poetry, that fragile thing / With rhyme and meter / with metaphors / With all its weeping willows / And what do you think of those "concretists" writing poems in shapes and with bits of words all stuck together / Poetry is like a gentle zephyr of delicate wanderings[19] and it should never ever touch upon politics / It must never ever use words like Fidel or Mao, it is enough for it to get involved in metaphysics or the erotic, because at times . . . / It doesn't matter, my child, poetry will continue laying sonnets, it's a dependable little hen . . . (*UR*, 51)

The voice here is that of a stuffy bourgeois, shocked by avant-garde poetry; another feature is a typographic trick—the slash rather than normal punctuation—which imparts a staccato quality to the text and thus may have some effect on the voice. A similar visual enhancement appears in a parallel passage a few pages beyond where the same "establishment" voice is decrying the technique of contemporary painters and sculptors:

> Don't you see? Today's painters: the very same thing. A LAW should be passed / And if the sale of tubes of paint were prohibited? / Don't kid yourself, these wretches would paint with anything—soot, leftover beer, spit mixed with cigarette butts / And the sculptors? To tame light, what a ridiculous idea. They were right to send Jules Le Parc out of France, that way he'll learn his lesson. Ah Rodin, now that was art. (*UR*, 55)

The final line of the original Spanish, "¡Ah Rodin, heso hera hel harte!" creates an additional special effect in its playful, deliberately incorrect use of the silent *h*. Readers may wonder if Cortázar wants us to pronounce the extra letter aloud, thus affecting some sort of high-flown tone suggestive of upper-class pretensions. Or is the author simply lampooning the overly fastidious bourgeois who feels the need to enhance or decorate simple words in order to give them more weight? At any rate, this "*h* game" is used in a similar manner in a number of other pieces and is closely related to the "mock serious" voice already discussed.[20]

In retrospect, "Noticias del mes de mayo" makes its point quite clearly, despite its very unusual nonlinear format. In almost every section of the text a great deal is going on more or less at the same time. Often the reader's eye can move over the page vertically, horizontally, or at random with equal effect. As Cortázar suggests, this can be considered a "porous" text. Finally, this piece is another wonderful example of the effectiveness of that catch phrase of the times—the medium is indeed the message. However, for those who remain faithful to *la Gran Polilla*—the "Great Stuffy Moth"—the essay will probably not be appreciated.

Collage, as seen in "Noticias," may be viewed as an extreme form of genre mixing. Less radical expressions of the same phenomenon, such as the incorporation of narrative elements into essentially expository writing, are found frequently in the essayistic work of Cortázar as well as others. In the context of Spanish American letters an important precursor of this kind of genre mixing was unquestionably the celebrated Argentine poet, essayist, and creator of fiction Jorge Luis Borges (1899–1986). Although most readers think of him primarily as a master of the short story, Borges produced a substantial corpus of essays and other short expository texts, many of which were quite traditional with regard to form, style, and theme. Moreover, he does not fit easily into an overview of the Spanish American essay since very few of his efforts in the genre dealt overtly with such canonical issues as identity, social questions, politics, New World versus European culture, and the like. Borges's relevancy to the present study lies in the fact that he was—albeit in subtle, understated ways—a clever and innovative proponent of genre mixing. As I have tried to show elsewhere,[21] several of his well-known *ficciones* may be considered essays rather than narratives. "Funes el memorioso," for example, though framed as an anecdotal first-person "story," is really a thinly veiled essay on memory and language. Similarly, the celebrated "Pierre Menard, autor del Quijote" can be viewed as an essay on certain problems of literary criticism (and, incidentally, of literary critics). Other examples from Borges's work could be offered; for our purposes, however, it is sufficient to take note of his important, though indirect, contribution to the new essay.

The work of Augusto Monterroso, discussed earlier in connection with the notion of the book as artifact, provides some interesting support for this relationship. In the first place, the Guatemalan-Mexican writer has made his debt to the Argentine master very clear in several essays, but most notably in a fine early tribute, "In illo tempore."[22] Second, and more important, Monterroso's remarkable tour de force, *Lo demás es silencio* (The rest is silence, 1978), reveals a number of very Borgesean features. First published in the Mortiz "Nueva Narrativa" series and subtitled "La vida y obra de Eduardo Torres" (The life and works of Edward Torres), the book is neither straight narrative nor a biocritical study of the apocryphal Torres. Rather, it is a mixed genre collection of essays, literary jokes, aphorisms, gratuitous addenda, and, of course, the tongue-in-cheek biography of Torres, presented from several differing viewpoints of friends and relatives. In the section on "selected works" of Edward Torres, Monterroso even includes a book review of his own earlier work, *La oveja negra y demás fábulas* (The black sheep and other fables, 1969), presumably written with an appropriately self-referential Latin citation, "asinus asinum fricat" (the jackass scratches the jackass). Thus, where Borges wrote reviews of nonexistent books, Monterroso has produced a review of his own work but ascribed it to a nonexistent author. *Lo demás es silencio* appears to have little if any message: like several other works considered here, it simply provides an amusing trip through a literary funhouse for both reader and author.

Another curious example of both genre mixing and Borgesean echoes is *El grafógrafo* (The graphographer, 1972) of Salvador Elizondo (1932–   ). This work, by one of Mexico's leading experimental prose writers, was, like Monterroso's *Lo demás es silencio*, published in the "Nueva Narrativa" series, though its essayistic character is easily as strong as its narrative content. A very self-conscious text, its individual pieces deal with the process of writing, with relationships between literary creation and painting, and with rather esoteric considerations of other semiotic issues. However, unlike the playful, folksy Monterroso, Elizondo's tone is typically abstract and obsessively sophisticated. A good example would be his bookish, effete essay, "Tractatus retórico-pictóricus," whose title alone would put off many readers. But perhaps the best case of narrative/expository blending in the collection is "Futuro imperfecto" (Future imperfect). Superficially this is a "story" in which the author is planning to submit a text—this text—to a journal[23] when a time-traveling stranger appears and shows him the future issue of the magazine in which this very piece will appear. Our author then thinks, "What if I decide now not to submit the text?" But he resists this temptation and observes that the "future" copy now available to him will be "a great help" in writing it![24] "Futuro imperfecto" is then—at least in my view—essentially a thinly disguised essay on time, the vanishing present, and the nature of narratives dealing with time travel.

However, once again it is Cortázar who provides the richest examples of genre mixing. Three works, *Historia de cronopios y famas*, *Un tal Lucas*, and *Vampiros multinacionales: una utopía realizable* (Multinational vampires: An attainable utopia, 1975), are, like Elizondo's *El grafógrafo* or Monterroso's *Lo demás es silencio*, books that few critics would accept as essays without serious reservations. Yet they all possess certain basic essayistic characteristics—they are expository texts in which the author has a position that he wishes to advance. Although narrative elements are present they are sufficiently weak or stylized to be easily forgotten. What the reader remembers is an authorial attitude, a viewpoint, or, in simplest terms, a message.

The first work is in effect a playful essay on human nature and social conventions in which Cortázar divides the world into his kind of people—the creative, high-flying, unconventional *cronopios*—and the dull, plodding "squares," or *famas*.[25] *Historia de cronopios y famas*, however, defies neat summation. First of all, it is hardly a serious book—were it so, Cortázar might be identified with the stodgy *famas*, one of whose major transgressions is taking things too seriously. Second, in addition to the main section, Cortázar in a sense prepares his readers by having them consider several essays in the "Instruction Manual" on "Unusual Occupations" and "Unstable Stuff." Without going into great detail, these supplementary sections are calculated to disturb the reader's sense of the ordinary by describing very common acts and occupations as if they were unusual, complicated, or mysterious. And perhaps they are: when we read his precise instructions for ascending a staircase or winding a watch we become aware of the surprising complexity of these acts. The "unusual occupations" describe, in a series of vignettes that often are almost short stories, the outlandish activities of a family dedicated to such pursuits as running a thoroughly absurd post office (where prizes and "give-aways" are offered) or constructing a backyard gallows which they never use and thus disappoint their neighbors. The final and most celebrated section of the volume presents, again in the form of brief vignettes, the ways of *cronopios*, *famas*, and *esperanzas*. Two of these three terms are existing Spanish words, though Cortázar's use of them is decidedly unorthodox: *esperanza* is the common noun for "hope"; *fama*, the word for "fame." However, neither (before Cortázar) has ever functioned as a generic noun describing a category of people. *Cronopio* is a complete invention, though its possible roots in *cronos* (time) and *opio* (opium or opiate) suggests the *cronopio*'s lackadaisical attitudes toward schedules, punctuality, and so on. At any rate, the most delightful sections of the entire work portray the *cronopios* in a variety of situations, often contrasted with their opposites, the *famas*. The piece on "Travel" is a good case in point. When *famas* visit a city, Cortázar tells us, they check and compare hotel prices, they register their possessions with the police, and they obtain a list of doctors and emergency services. By contrast, "when *cronopios* go on a trip they find that all the hotels are filled up, the trains have already left, it is raining buckets and taxis don't want to pick them up, either that or they charge them exorbitant prices. The *cronopios* are not disheartened ... When they manage, finally, to find a bed and are ready to go to sleep, they say to one another, 'What a beautiful city, what a very beautiful city!' And all night long they dream that high parties are being given at the hotel and that they are invited."[26] It may do Cortázar an injustice to cite other examples of the *cronopio-fama* polarity, since much in this text resists neat, schematic analysis. The nature of the less-developed, somewhat lethargic *esperanzas* blurs the image considerably: similarly, many small details in the work remain charmingly undecipherable. What, for example, is the significance of the names given the *cronopio*'s dances of exaltation, *tregua* (truce), *respite* (?), or *catalá* (Catalan)?

A few words will suffice regarding Cortázar's *Vampiros multinacionales: una utopía realizable*, or, as its cover page proclaims, *Fantomas contra los vampiros multinacionales*. A genuine literary curiosity, this seventy-seven-page production is in effect a narrative text supplemented by some eight pages of comic strips along with other graphic enhancements and an appendix consisting of a detailed report describing the findings of the second Russell Tribunal (held in January 1975 in Brussels for the purpose of investigating the violation of political and human rights in Latin America). Despite the seriousness of the work's political message, its comic book cover is reminiscent of *Superman* or, better, *Captain Marvel*. The comic strip sections (presumably the narrator, i.e., Cortázar himself, is reading this comic book while on the train from Brussels, where he actually served as a member of the tribunal) recount the campaign of the superhero "Fantomas" against the forces of evil; namely, international big business and the United States. These elements apparently have conspired to eliminate high culture throughout the world by burning down libraries and threatening the lives of writers—especially politically conscious writers. Specific targets of Cortázar's outrage are Henry Kissinger, the CIA, the ITT corporation, and the United States's role in ousting Allende as president of Chile. The few fictitious characters in the work are complemented by a number of very real literary celebrities—Susan Sontag, Octavio Paz, Alberto Moravia, Carlos Fuentes—who appear both in the comic strip and in the regular text. Cortázar himself is a primary figure as the internal, active narrator. He has phone conversations with his literary colleagues and he discusses his campaign with the fictional Fantomas. He also appears in the comic strip, modestly labeled as "a great Argentine writer." In the normal text he even describes his erotic fantasies while flirting with an attractive blond in his train compartment. While *Vampiros* has strong narrative elements, the "story"—such as it is— seems deliberately trivial: considered as an essay, however, it presents a clear message laden with strong moral indictment. Cortázar, as noted, wishes to condemn the United States's manipulation of Latin America and its support of repressive regimes. But he also strives to awaken Latin American intellectuals to their responsibilities. Like Fantomas, they are often victims of their own illusions—the superhero's symbolic struggle against the burning of books is merely *un gran engaño*, a great deception, since he is only fighting a superficial aspect of the multinationals' plan. Thus, unless writers view their activity in proper perspective, they too will be deceived: as Susan Sontag asks the author, "What good are books in comparison to those who read them, Julio? Of what use are entire libraries if they are only available to a few? This . . . is a trap for intellectuals. The loss of a single book bothers us more than hunger in Ethiopia."[27] In sum, this strange mixture of serious concern and pop-art jauntiness may, provided one accepts a very flexible definition of the genre, be considered an essay. But beyond any literary considerations one wonders just why Cortázar produced the hybrid. What audience did he have in mind? Did he really believe that *Vampiros* could be an effective weapon in the struggle against exploitation and repression?

These questions need not be raised in reference to his charming, subtly offbeat work of 1979. *Un tal Lucas* has gone through a number of printings and has been published in English translation in a major house.[28] The book is divided into three sections: the first and last consist of short sketches describing Lucas's adventures (or misadventures), attitudes, likes, phobias, and so on, while the middle section features miscellaneous mini-essays on a variety of topics. Although there is no overall unifying structure, all three parts are held together by the personality of Lucas—even the random thoughts of the second section seem to represent the workings of his eccentric mind. Essentially cronopian, Lucas is nonetheless rather timid and basically low key. Rather than do violence to the establishment, he quietly gnaws away at reality and accepted conventions. In one piece, for example, he subverts the rigidity of normal hospital procedures by politely requesting the staff to rearrange his entire room to accommodate a single daisy displayed in a glass of water. Having accomplished this, he confesses that he really doesn't like daisies and so he simply throws the flower out the window (*UTL*, 57–59). The foregoing sketch clearly has a strong narrative element, but others are primarily expository.

The three writers I have chosen to illustrate how genre mixing can be exploited for essayistic purposes—Monterroso, Elizondo, and, above all, Cortázar—do not represent isolated cases of this phenomenon. Several others merit at least passing mention. Uruguayan leftist Eduardo Galeano (whose ideas were examined in chapters 2 and 3) incorporates narrative and autobiographical touches in much of his writing, but especially in his very personal—and very political—collection *Días y noches de amor y guerra*; Peruvian writer of fiction Julio Ramón Ribeyro, in his "spiritual self-portrait" *Prosas apátridas* (Expatriate prose, 1975), combines memoirs, vignettes, and narrative elements to produce a remarkable record of geographic and personal exile; and finally, Alejandro Rossi of Venezuela and Mexico reflects strong Borgesean affinities in his collection of traditional essays and essayistic narratives, *Manual del distraído* (Manual of a distracted man, 1978).

THE ESSAY AS POETRY

One of the richest forms of genre mixing and one that has many antecedents in Hispanic as well as other literatures is the recourse to an essentially poetic mode—to lyrical, intensely emotional, often highly figurative language—to serve the ends of narrative or expository writing. What I am trying to describe here, poetic prose, has been an important component of the new essay. A number of authors that we have examined have on occasion produced texts which could be considered under this rubric. Two may well be genuine masters of this kind of writing: Octavio Paz and Julio Cortázar. That Paz should incorporate poetry into his work should come as no surprise given the fact that he is regarded as one of the hemisphere's major poets; indeed, even in his earliest essayistic prose, as well as in his *Laberinto de la soledad*, the lyrical element was strong. Cortázar, while he has written some poetry, is primarily a prose writer, though a number of the pieces in *Ultimo round* and *Vuelta al día* have a definite poetic character. The two essayistic texts which best illustrate my point are not found among the most widely read works of either writer: they are Paz's *El mono gramático* (*The Monkey Grammarian*, 1974)[29] and Cortázar's *Prosa del observatorio* (Prose from the observatory, 1972). As we shall see, there are tenuous links between the two: both are, in part, inspired by a fascination with Indian culture and both explore the possibilities of analogic thinking.

El mono gramático is not an easy work to describe. As Jason Wilson, an astute commentator on Paz, observes, "For a critic to retrace the process of Paz's poetics . . . would be to rewrite *El mono gramático*. To regroup the text according to categories and themes would be to ignore the crucial temporal structure.

The critic is left clutching and stressing elements wrenched from a process."[30] Paz prefaces the text with a quotation from *The Classical Dictionary of Hindu Mythology* describing Hanuman (or Hanumat), a mythical "monkey chief," a kind of super anthropoid, who was celebrated for being very learned and for being "the ninth author of grammar." This creature, the Monkey Grammarian, is referred to briefly and only occasionally, though his perspective, his symbolic force, and his physical image—an altar in the courtyard in the crumbling palace of the Indian city of Galta—provide one of the foci of the text. *El mono gramático* is, in broadest terms, a highly lyrical philosophical essay on language and poetics. Paz's method is circular rather than linear and his basic tone is meditative.

The work begins with a series of alternating chapters in which the author describes first the journey or path to Galta and then his thoughts on gazing upon a boreal thicket of birches, aspens, and ashes seen from his Cambridge window.[31] The Galta sequences appear to be remembered while the Cambridge material represents the authorial here and now—the text's point of departure. The two perspectives are, however, essentially the same, since one describes a journey through space—the path to Galta, its palace and inner courtyard—and the other the author's struggle in his Cambridge study to produce a text, to shape the literary artifact. As he notes in chapter 3, "Galta is not here: it is awaiting me at the end of this phrase" (*MG*, 11). As this remark indicates, *El mono gramático* is an intensely self-conscious text. Indeed, what Paz is doing here is metaliterary—he is writing about writing:

> I feel the same perplexity as when confronted with its [Galta's] hilltops leveled off by centuries of wind and its yellowed plains on which . . . the dust clouds rise. Reddish, grayish, or dusky apparitions that suddenly come forth like a waterspout or geyser . . . Phantoms that dance like whirling dervishes, that advance, retreat, fall motionless . . . apparitions without substance, ceremonies of dust and air. What I am writing is also a ceremony, the whirling of a word that disappears as it circles round and round. I am erecting towers of air. (*MG*, 12)

The foregoing hints at another basic preoccupation that informs the entire essay: the frustration of the writer facing the impossible task of apprehending reality, especially the reality of the present moment, by means of language. Like Zeno the Eleatic, Chinese philosopher Hui Shih, or Borges (if we wish a Spanish American example), Paz is acutely aware that fixity is illusory, that once we write or say "now" it is history; thus his fourth chapter is devoted to a vertiginous analysis of its opening statement, "fixity is always momentary" (*MG*, 17).

The most intense sections of the text describe, or evoke, the path to Galta. This journey, while very real (it is illustrated by photos), is enhanced by rich symbolic suggestions: the underlying notion that the act of writing is tantamount to finding a pathway through the jungle of textual possibilities; the traditional Oriental peregrination in search of enlightenment and the mythic voyage of Hanuman, charged with creative semen, across the seas. The latter vision is evoked by the author's contemplation of "a wall stained with damp patches and with traces of paint, most likely . . . a landscape, not that of Galta but another" (*MG*, 31). This vision triggers a mountain scene or "a sea shaken with violent spasms," dominated by the body of the Monkey Grammarian, "the elephant of monkeys, the lion, the bull of simians" who is seen swimming against wind and storm, all the while resisting huge "lascivious" beasts that are "eager to devour the great monkey, eager to copulate with the chaste simian, to break open his great hermetically sealed jars full of semen accumulated over the centuries and centuries of abstinence, eager to broadcast the virile substance to the four points of the compass, to disseminate it, to dispense being" (*MG*, 33). This very strange segment of the text ends with the author's musings upon returning to the paint-splattered Galta wall: "perhaps there is painted here everything that Hanuman did and saw there after having bounded across the sea in one leap—an indecipherable jumble of lines, strokes, spirals, mad maps, grotesque stories, the discourse of monsoons inscribed in the crumbling wall" (*MG*, 33–34).

The powerful imagery of the foregoing is perhaps Paz's way of preparing the reader for chapter 7, in my view one of the most impressive examples of erotic poetic prose to be found in contemporary Spanish American letters. It can only be cited in its entirety:

An indecipherable thicket of lines, strokes, spirals, maps: the discourse of fire on the wall. A motionless surface traversed by a flickering brightness: the shimmer of transparent water on the still bottom of the spring illuminated by invisible reflectors. A motionless surface on which the fire projects silent, fleeting, heavy shadows: beneath the ripples of the crystal-clear water dark phantoms swiftly slither. One, two, three, four black rays emerge from a black sun, grow longer, advance, occupy the whole of space, which oscillates and undulates, they fuse, form once again the dark sun of which they were born, emerge once again from this sun—like the fingers of a hand that opens, closes, and opens once again to transform itself into a fig leaf, a trefoil, a profusion of black wings, before vanishing altogether. A cascade of water silently plunges over the smooth walls of a dam. A charred moon rises out of a gaping abyss. A boat with billowing sails sends forth roots overhead, capsizes, becomes an inverted tree. Garments that fly in the air above a landscape of hills made of lampblack. Drifting continents, oceans in eruption. Surging waters, wave upon wave. The wind scatters the weightless rocks. A telamon shatters to bits. Birds again, fishes again. The shadows lock in embrace and cover the entire wall. They draw apart. Bubbles in the center of the liquid surface, concentric circles, submerged bells tolling in the depths. Splendor removes her garments with one hand, without letting go of her partner's rod with the other. As she strips naked, the fire on the hearth clothes her in copper-colored reflections. She has dropped her garments to one side and is swimming through the shadows. The light of the fire coils about Splendor's ankles, mounts between her thighs, illuminates her pubis and belly. The sun-colored water wets her fleecy mound and pene-trates the lips of her vulva. The tempered tongue of the flames on the moist pudenda; the tongue enters and blindly gropes its way along the palpitating walls. The many-fingered water opens the valves and rubs the stubborn erectile button hidden amid dripping folds. The reflec-tions, the flames, the waves lock in embrace and draw apart. Quivering shadows above the space that pants like an animal, shadows of a double butterfly that opens, closes, opens its wings. Knots. The surging waves rise and fall on Splendor's reclining body. The shadow of an animal drinking in shadows between the parted legs of the young woman. Water: shadow; light: silence. Light: water; shadow: silence. Silence: water; light: shadow. (*MG*, 38–40)

The relationship of these erotic elements and especially the person of "Splendor" to the complete work defies easy explanation. The text appears to be infused with intertwining conceptual vines: writing becomes not only a ritualistic journey but may also be an erotic penetration through a "thicket," toward a "gateway," and into an inner courtyard. All these metaphoric possi-bilities appear to be fused in the interdependent descriptions of Galta's archi-tecture and the act of copulation. Splendor herself is an extremely problematic figure. At times she seems to be the author's companion, a kind of Beatrice accompanying him on his path to Galta and on his quest for enlightenment. However, at other times, as in the intensely erotic chapter 11, the author pre-sents her from a third-person perspective making love by firelight with a vaguely described male. Although this scene is extremely graphic, the reality of Splendor and the sex act is undermined by Paz's semiotic musings:

> He returns to Splendor's side and watches the reflections of the fire glide over her body. Garments of light, garments of water: her nakedness is more naked. He can now see her and grasp the whole of her. Before he had glimpsed only bits and pieces of her: a thigh, an elbow, the palm of a hand, a foot, a knee, an ear nestling in a lock of damp hair, an eye between eyelashes, the softness of backs of knees and insides of thighs reaching up as far as the dark zone rough to the touch, the wet black thicket between his fingers, the tongue between the teeth and the lips, a body more felt than seen, a body made of pieces of a body, regions of wetness or dryness, open or bosky areas, mounds or clefts, never the body, only its parts, each part a momentary totality in turn immediately split apart, a body segmented, quartered, carved up, chunks of ear ankle groin breast fingernail, each piece a sign of the body of bodies, each part whole and entire, each sign an image that appears and burns until it consumes itself, each image a chain of vibrations, each vibration the perception of a sensation that dies away, millions of bodies in each vibration, millions of universes in each body, a rain of universes on the body of Splendor which is not a body but the river of signs of her body . . . (*MG*, 66–67)

Whatever she may be (love goddess, muse, companion, or merely a focus of signs), she, like virtually all else in the text, functions in an essentially analogic manner. As Jason Wilson has suggested, in this work everything is "like" everything else. Recalling Paz's tremendous debt to Breton and the surrealist tradition, he notes: "André Breton's magic word *comme* (like) is at the heart of Paz's poetics: he reveals the analogies as a 'system of mirrors' . . . The 'étreinte des corps' (embrace of bodies) and the notion that 'words make love' . . . both underpin the erotic imagery of *comme*."[32] Paz himself frequently corroborates this view, as when in chapter 25 he tells us, "the path is writing and writing is a body and a body is bodies. . . . the body is always somewhere beyond the body. On touching it divides itself (like a text) into portions that are momentary sensations: a sensation that is a perception of a thigh, an earlobe, a nipple, a fingernail, a warm patch of groin . . . The body that we embrace is a river of metamorphoses" (*MG*, 142).

Given the nature of this analogic process, it would seem almost sacrilegious to state what the "central theme" or "message" of *El mono gramático* might be. Nonetheless, I am persuaded to return to my original point: this essay, prose

poem, or "treatise," as Paz himself calls it, is an explication/demonstration/
meditation on the author's fundamental views regarding the nature and limitations of the creative act known as writing. His statements—and images—
describing this process are tinged with frustration, perhaps desperation, not
unlike an unfulfilled sexual hunger: "writing is a search for the meaning that
writing itself violently expels. At the end of the search meaning evaporates and
reveals to us a reality that literally is meaningless. What remains? The twofold
movement of writing: a journey in the direction of meaning, a dissipation of
meaning. An allegory of mortality: these phrases that I write, this path that I
invent as I endeavor to describe the path that leads to Galta, become blurred,
dissolve as I write: I never reach the end" (*MG*, 133–134). Very near the book's
conclusion Paz sheds even more light on the nature of *El mono gramático*:

> Today I realize that my text was not going anywhere—except to meet
> itself. I also perceive that repetitions are metaphors and that reitera-
> tions are analogies: a system of mirrors that little by little have revealed
> another text. In this text Hanuman contemplates the garden of Ravana
> like a page of calligraphy, like the harem of the same Ravana . . . like
> this page in which the swaying motions of the beeches in the grove op-
> posite my window accumulate on this page like the shadows of two
> lovers . . . like the stains of monsoon rains on a ruined palace . . . of the
> abandoned town of Galta, like . . . the wave upon wave of a multitude
> contemplated . . . by hundreds of monkeys . . . like a metaphor of the
> path and the pilgrimage to the sanctuary like the final dissolution of
> the path and the convergence of all the texts in this paragraph like a
> metaphor of the embrace of bodies. Analogy: universal transparency:
> seeing is this that. (*MG*, 157–159)

Cortázar's *Prosa del observatorio,* our second text illustrating the outer bound-
ary of the essay as it approaches poetry, is in some ways similar to Paz's work.
Like the *Mono gramático,* Cortázar's piece relies heavily on analogy and has
some erotic undercurrents, and, by coincidence, half the work is set in India.
Containing some eighty pages of text and accompanied by his own photographs, it is apparently his longest single essay. Unlike *Ultimo round* or *La vuelta*
this is a tightly integrated, unified work instead of being collagelike in structure.
Typically Cortazarian, the essay's essential meaning is revealed only gradually
to readers psychologically set to collaborate with the author. *Prosa del observatorio* is an "image" built upon two substantive elements: a technical description of the reproductive cycle and migration pattern of the Atlantic eel and a
photographically illustrated text describing the astronomical observatory of a

relatively obscure Indian sultan, Jai Singh.[33] These seemingly disparate items have much in common: the millions of tiny newly hatched eels mysteriously guided from the sea to the rivers and the uncountable stars which Jai Singh hopes to measure, organize, and somehow understand both provide examples of phenomena which man attempts to make rational by means of his intellect through "la Dama Ciencia," to use Cortázar's own phrase. However, the message of *Prosa del observatorio* seems to transcend this point: beyond science and rationality, beyond "Madam Science and her retinue, morality, the cities, society"[34] lies another realm (and one not unfamiliar to readers of Paz), that of "that which is open, the red-headed night, the zones of excess, the spirit of clowns, of acrobats, of sleep-walkers" (*PO*, 61). In some obscure, poetically conceived fashion Cortázar desires that these two opposing spheres be reconciled. Thus, he ends the essay with the hope that "conciliation is possible, where obverse and reverse will no longer be opposites, where man will be able to take his place in that joyful dance that we will some day call reality" (*PO*, 79). The foregoing summary of the essay's content or "message" is perhaps overly schematicized, since intertwined with the central idea are a number of very Cortazarian, and again very Pazian, dualities: that which is open versus that which is closed, Madam Science versus the "red-headed night," and the world as it is versus the utopia to be engendered by revolution. In addition, an undercurrent of eroticism and a sense of the interrelatedness of all things permeate the text.

To appreciate *Prosa del observatorio* fully the reader must, however, abandon the tendency to educe from it neatly formulated statements of fact or viewpoint. Rather, one must accept the author's invitation to become enmeshed in the rhythm, in the textual flow of the piece, itself suggestive of the cosmic forces that Cortázar is attempting to apprehend. The first few pages amply illustrate the text's tone, authorial voice, rhythmic patterns, and other stylistic features:

> That hour that on occasion may arrive beyond all hours, a hole in the net of time, that way of being between not on top of or behind but between, that orifice hour that comes under the protection of other hours, of uncountable life with its front hours and side hours, its time for everything, its things at the right time, being in a hotel room, or on a station platform, looking at a shop window a dog perhaps holding you in my arms, love in the afternoon, at siesta, glimpsing through that clear spot the door that opens on the terrace, seeing in a green flash the blouse you took off to give me the light salt that trembles on your breasts, and without warning, without unnecessary indications of

change, in a café of the Latin Quarter, or in the last sequence of a Pabst film, a partition no longer set in proper place, an access between two occupations installed in the niche of time, in the beehive day, in this way or in another way (in the shower, in the middle of the street, in a sonata, in a telegram) to touch something that is not sustained by one's senses, that break in continuity, just so, sliding so, the eels, for example, the sargasso region, the eels and also the machines of marble, the Jai Singh night drinking a flow of stars, the observatories beneath the Jaipur and Delhi moon, the black ribbon of migration, the eels right out on the street or in the orchestra seats of a theater, revealing themselves to those who would follow them from the marble machines, that fellow who no longer looks at his watch in the Paris night; just simply a Moebius strip of eels and of marble machines, what flows in a lone, wild word searching for itself, which also sets off the migration of a verb from Sargasso Seas of time and fortuitous semantics: discourse, the Atlantic eels and eel words, lightening flashes of marble and the machines of Jai Singh, he who observes the stars and the eels, the Moebius strip circulating within itself, in the ocean, in Jaipur, fulfilling itself again without repetition, being like what marble is, what the eel is: you probably understand that nothing of this can be said from sidewalks or chairs or city theater stages. (*PO*, 7–11)

The poetic character of the text is seen in the opening series of "thats," *esas*, complemented by the repetition of the verb *estar*, in other alliterations, and in the word groups punctuated only by commas. In addition, the juxtaposition of highly figurative language ("hole in the net of time," "the niche of time," "the night drinking a flow of stars," etc.) with brief but very literal descriptions ("being in a hotel room," "a café in the Latin Quarter") creates vertiginous effects reminiscent of surreal art. The images ebb and flow; the mass of eels blends into a street mob or the audience of a theater; sign and that which is signified lose their identity as even words become eels; readers are asked to surrender themselves to Jai Singh's marble machinery, to be part of the Moebius strip which itself may be the text—only in this way, perhaps, will this remarkable piece of writing have meaning.

The striking similarity with Paz's *El mono gramático* becomes very apparent when individual elements within the two texts are compared. The fleeting, almost subliminal images, a café in the Latin Quarter for Cortázar and the view of the trees from his Cambridge window for Paz, become superimposed upon other realities: the swarm of spermlike eels in the Atlantic or the stains on the walls of Galta. The attempt to illumine writing/language in analogic terms is as strong in Cortázar's essay as it is in Paz's. Note, in the passage cited above, this thing that already "flows in a lone, wild word searching for itself, which also sets off the migration of a verb from Sargasso Seas of time and fortuitous semantics: discourse, the Atlantic eels and eel words." Note also the sense of circularity, of returning to the starting point, that characterizes both works: Paz's clear realization, stated in his conclusion, that his essay "was not going anywhere—except to meet itself" and Cortázar's provocative description of his text as a Moebius strip, "circulating within itself."

THE SELF-CONSCIOUS ESSAYIST

In the present chapter I have attempted to make my case for the new essay by examining a variety of formal features and techniques that distinguish essayistic writing of recent decades from traditional work in the genre: manipulation of authorial voice, collage, genre mixing, unusual formatting, and the use of poetic prose. One of the most interesting, and perhaps most significant, aspects of this activity is the fact that many of the new essayists reveal an acute awareness of what some might consider their literary transgressions. In sum, they are very self-conscious writers who often share their concerns regarding this craft with their readers. Other examples of this phenomenon are not hard to find.

Gabriel Zaid, in the opening lines of his *Como leer en bicicleta*, considers the ill-defined boundaries of the genre and confesses: "when I began to write these articles, my objective was exploratory: to assay the essay itself" (*CLB*, 8). He goes on to note that he was often bored by ordinary expository prose: "I was fed up with reading reviews and essays that did not answer to my needs as a reader—could this infamous genre really become 'creative'?" (*CLB*, 8). Others, Alejandro Rossi, for example, simply alert their readers to expect unconventional, generic hybrids in their texts. Thus, early in his *Manual del distraído* he states, "The reader will find here more or less canonical essays as well as those that seem more like narratives; he will also discover narratives that include essayistic elements."[35] In an entirely different tone, Salvador Elizondo begins his cleverly titled *El grafógrafo* with a statement that pushes the notion of authorial self-consciousness to its ultimate limits: "I write. I write that I am writing. Mentally I see myself writing that I am writing and I also can see myself seeing that I am writing . . . And I see myself remembering that I see myself writing and I remember seeing myself remember that I was writing . . . I can also imagine myself writing that I had written that I was imagining myself writing that I see myself writing that I am writing."[36] Though somewhat less flamboyant, both Paz and Cortázar reveal a great deal of authorial self-consciousness along with the attending desire to have the reader participate in the creative process. One of Paz's best examples of self-conscious writing is, not surprisingly, found in the text we have just examined, *El mono gramático*. Throughout the book Paz ponders what he is trying to do while sharing his reflections with his readers. Note again the opening of the fourth chapter: "fixity is always momentary. But how can it *always* be so? If it were, it would not be momentary—or would not be fixity. What did I mean by that phrase? I probably had in mind the opposition between motion and motionless. . . . My phrase tends to dissolve this opposition and hence represents a sly violation of the principle of identity. . . . A little rhetorical trick intended to give an air of plausibility to my violation of the rules of logic" (*MG*, 17). Other examples from the same text could be offered.

In a slightly different manner Cortázar strives to articulate his problems as a writer and his strategies for overcoming them. Two excellent examples may be found in *Ultimo round*, "La muñeca rota" (The broken doll) and "/que sepa abrir la puerta para ir a jugar." The former, an attempt to explicate the conjunction of existential and aesthetic forces that produce a text, results in a complex essay that sheds considerable light on the workings of Cortázar's highly analogic mind. The second piece, a fascinating meditation on the nature of erotic literature, merits more detailed attention. The subject matter of "/que sepa abrir la puerta para ir a jugar" has already been noted in chapter 2. It will be recalled that the thrust of this essay is that the inhibitions felt by Latin American writers when they attempt to produce erotic literature can be traced to the perception of themselves as representatives of a "colonial," "dependent," or Third World area. What must be stressed at this point, however, is that this essay is also a revealing example of authorial self-consciousness. In it Cortázar confesses his problems when trying to write genuinely erotic literature: "fear continues to deflect our compass needles; in all of my work I have never, not even once, been able to write the word *concha* (cunt), which on at least two occasions I needed more than my cigarettes" (*UR*, 153). It is significant, moreover, that in the same piece Cortázar's illustrations of erotic texts are either in the original French or English, never in Spanish translations.

This revelation of self-consciousness, tinged by doubt concerning one's identity (as a writer, as an individual, as a part of a wider culture), underlies a great deal of contemporary Spanish American writing. Yet the willingness of essayists (and novelists) to experiment, to innovate, to break generic molds is indicative that these writers represent a growing movement toward literary and cultural self-confidence; symbolic, perhaps, of the hemisphere's coming of age. Their sense of being members of the "marginal" or "dependent" Third World—in aesthetic as well as political terms—has been overcome to a considerable degree. Yet the hesitancy with which they have approached certain kinds of writing—eroticism and the not completely unrelated area of humor—is also indicative that this process has not fully evolved. But important steps have been taken, and the work of the most impressive essayists of the group (again Octavio Paz comes to mind) suggests that the "colonial" or peripheral status of Spanish American letters has already been transcended.

Even somewhat lesser-known essayists have, I think, pointed toward this coming of age. For example, Gabriel Zaid, despite his wry humor and fondness for literary gamesmanship, has produced several impressive essays which set forth fresh and remarkably fruitful views of the relationship of Spanish America to its Old World roots. One such text is "Problemas de una cultura matriotera" (Problems of a matriarchal culture), in which he suggests that it is time for Mexico (though I find no difficulty in applying his thinking to other areas of Latin America) to rid itself of its outmoded fixations as an "abandoned child" dependent upon a protective but passive mother figure—that Mexicans stop thinking of themselves as "impotent victims" of the conquistador or, in contemporary terms, of great powers such as the United States. He urges his compatriots to recognize that their roots lie in the culture of the Old World: in the symbology of his text, this means that Mexicans accept their "father"—Europe—as well as their indigenous mother. This of course does not imply a denial of the autochthonous elements in the culture, nor does it mean that by accepting the historical connections with Golden Age Spain or France of the enlightenment they will perpetuate the hemisphere's status as a colonial outpost, as a poor relative eating the crumbs off the banquet table of Eurocentric culture (*CLB*, 143). Rather, his message is that Mexico accept the active "paternal" element—Western civilization in the broadest sense—that has been decisive in shaping New World society since the fifteenth century. Zaid is no traditional Europeanist: this acceptance must be understood as a challenge, as an invitation to participate in and to contribute toward Western civilization: "it is high time to be heirs of our own works. To reject our paternity at this point is to reject ourselves, it is to deny our history, to refuse to take charge of it . . . [it is to deny] the dream of modifying the Europeans themselves by intervening as active agents, rather than being objects of their curiosity or applause" (*CLB*, 147–148).

Conclusions

We may now refine and summarize what was chosen as the informing concept of this study, the notion of dissent. To do this, several connotations of this term must be kept in mind. Perhaps the most obvious kind of dissent we have seen in our essayists is on the purely political level—criticism, disagreement, or protest against nations, political parties, or what we have come to call the establishment. Writing of this kind has, all would agree, a long tradition in Spanish America as elsewhere. Similarly, dissent regarding social practices and taboos—the critique of sexual mores and inhibitions discussed in chapter 2, for example—is hardly new, though it becomes more strident during the period under examination. A somewhat different situation can be seen in the dissent noted in chapter 3. Here the essayists take issue with trends accepted by a wide range of people—by governments, by parties, and, most important, by the man in the street. When they question the pursuit of progress for its own sake, the cult of development, or the view of urban life as the acme of civilization, they are challenging some of the twentieth century's most cherished articles of faith. The critique of ideology, examined in our fourth chapter, may well be one of the most radical forms of dissent. Though the primary target of the anti-ideologues has been Marxism, the implications of their attack go beyond partisan lines: carried to ultimate conclusions, their views suggest some different ways of looking at the relationship between ideas and reality. Finally, in our last chapter, the notion of dissent is interpreted in terms of formal innovations, literary techniques, textual stratagems, and stylistics. We saw, moreover, that a number of writers studied are very aware of their aesthetic dissent and that this self-consciousness has implications that transcend purely literary considerations. In effect, it can be linked with fundamental issues of identity and the relationship of the New World to the Old. Thus, the conclusion of the chapter suggests that this spirit of aesthetic boldness may be interpreted as a sign of the hemisphere's coming of age.

It could be argued that much of the dissent found in Spanish American essayists of the period simply parallels general trends observable throughout the Western world. It would not be difficult to find non-Hispanic writers who have challenged traditional ideas regarding the nature of revolution, who have questioned social patterns, who have analyzed the generational strife of the sixties, who have spoken out against the nearly universal infatuation with tech- notopias, and who have disputed the sanity of forcing political or economic decisions to fit the mold of abstract ideology. Last, my characterization of the "new essay" can easily be seen in terms of a pervasive movement evident in European and North American letters: postmodernism. Admittedly ill- defined,[1] the new aesthetic of the late twentieth century accommodates the formal features of the new essay quite easily: genre mixing, violations of tra- ditional frames, nonlinear exposition, analogic thinking, the printed page as a semiotic artifact, and so on.

The fact that our essayists have been concerned about the same issues—and express themselves in a similar manner—as their counterparts elsewhere is a further indication that Spanish America is well on its way to transcending its former status as a vibrant, picturesque, but essentially peripheral cultural zone. Indeed, writers like Paz, Borges, and the major novelists of the *nueva narrativa* have been recognized universally as innovative masters of contemporary let- ters. In short, the best of Ibero-American writing is no longer derivative, but, rather, contributory to the mainstream of Western literature. However, this does not mean that it has lost its distinctive character nor does it imply that long-standing Spanish American concerns are no longer lurking just below the surface. The essayists we have studied illustrate this quite well. The theme of identity—who we are, where we came from, and where we are going—contin- ues, albeit expressed somewhat differently than it was earlier, as an important concern of a number of writers, though it is not as dominant a preoccupation as it was forty or fifty years ago.[2] Gabriel Zaid's "Problemas de una cultura matriotera" is a good case in point and is also illustrative of newer perspectives on an old theme. Even a work such as Monsiváis's *Amor perdido* can be viewed as an attempt to interpret the Mexican essence in a period when international, "cosmopolite" forces were making tremendous inroads on Mexican life. Simi- larly, Octavio Paz, years after his ground-breaking study, *El laberinto de la so- ledad,* has continued to probe the question of identity in the context of recent situations, as, for example, in his *Posdata.* To a lesser degree contemporary

Argentine essayists such as Sebreli, Mafud, and Kusch have carried on the work of earlier writers—Martínez Estrada or Mallea—in attempting to define *argentinedad.*

The Mexicans, nonetheless, appear to have done more with the identity question and, for that matter, with virtually all the other issues examined in this study than has any other group. This simple fact must be considered as one of our inevitable conclusions: Mexico has had more essayists, more essay-istic debate, and very probably a richer essayistic tradition than any other Span-ish American nation. In sum, Mexican essayists do not work in a vacuum: thus, when a writer such as Zaid probes the question of cultural origins and identity, his work comes as a kind of expanded footnote to a century-long discussion of these matters in the works of Octavio Paz, Alfonso Reyes, Samuel Ramos, José Vasconcelos, Justo Sierra, and others.[3] Moreover, Mexican essayists have been especially fortunate in having at their disposal a wide range of publications in which issues might be aired, polemics might be sustained, and, in a word, essays might be essayed.[4] Few other Latin American nations are comparable in this regard, though Argentina—at times—would provide a somewhat similar en-vironment. Finally, though no one could argue that Mexico has an ideal climate for intellectual activity, by contrast with many other countries, interference with free expression of opinion and political violence have been minimal for a good part of the postrevolutionary period. Moreover, when the political estab-lishment does become overbearing, writers feel free to criticize and to name names with considerable assurance that they will not be imprisoned or forced to flee the country. It is significant that there have been virtually no Mexicans among the ranks of what has become a twentieth-century stereotype: the Latin American in involuntary exile. The contrast with writers of other major coun-tries—Chile, Cuba, Peru, Argentina—is obvious.

One of the central concerns of Spanish American essayists continues to be the relationship with North America. Since the turn of the century the many questions revolving about the political, economic, and cultural inroads of the United States—*el coloso del Norte*, as it was often called at the time—concerned writers such as Manuel Ugarte, Rufino Blanco Fombona, José Martí, and, most notably, José Enrique Rodó. The rather nonideological anti-Yankeeism of this early generation became more sharply focused after the 1920s, when Marxist thought, as seen in the work of radical essayists such as Peruvian José Carlos Mariátegui, Cuba's Juan Marinello, and others led to a more doctrinaire cri-tique of the colossus of the North. By the postwar period and especially with the advent of the Cuban revolution of Fidel Castro, it is safe to say that a pervasive anti-Yankeeism—typically colored by Marxist/nationalist ideology—had become very evident throughout the hemisphere as a canonical position among writers, intellectuals in general, and especially members of the academic community. Much of this has changed. It would be overstating the case to claim that since the late 1960s intellectuals have effected a 180-degree turn in their attitudes toward the United States, yet the evidence provided by the present study suggests that a number of the hemisphere's strongest voices have rejected much of the simplistic anti-Yankeeism of the recent past. It would be difficult to determine whether this shift has come about as a by-product of the general critique of ideology, as a reaction to the repressive policies evident in Marxist regimes, as a result of the growing perception that Western economic systems, despite their flaws and injustices, have been more effective than state-controlled structures, or as a combination of all these factors. The fact remains that a host of major writers—Vargas Llosa, Paz, Jorge Edwards, Sábato, Fuentes—have become much more balanced, and at times quite positive, in their assessment of North American society, values, and even politics. Again, this does not mean that they accept this country's culture or policies without question. Vargas Llosa has, for example, been quite critical of the United States's activities in Central America, and Octavio Paz, in my view, will never reconcile himself to certain basic North American values. We have also seen ample evidence that the cult of technology, rampant *desarrollismo*, and progress for progress' sake—attitudes typical of the Yankee mainstream—have not gone unchallenged.

Several years ago a student of Spanish American letters suggested that the area's essay was "in hibernation." Others have doubted that the late twentieth century could produce essayists comparable to such masters of the genre as Sarmiento, Rodó, or Reyes. The present study, it is hoped, has helped dispel these highly exaggerated rumors that the Spanish American essay is dead, or even sleeping. The genre, though it may be in the guise of a magazine article or a piece in a Sunday newspaper supplement, is apparently alive and well. Essayists such as Octavio Paz or Mario Vargas Llosa continue to publish widely read, widely discussed, magnificently crafted texts, and even lesser-known writers such as Carlos Rangel, Jorge Edwards, or Fernández Retamar can create a storm of debate with their highly controversial work. Other cases might be cited: the fact is that this genre, while it typically remains faithful to the spirit and intent of its European founders (those two undaunted dissenters, Montaigne and Bacon), persists as a living, constantly changing, and aesthetically exciting expression of a continent's essence.

Notes

I. INTRODUCTION

1. Scholes and Klaus, *Elements of the Essay*, p. 46.

2. Among the many names that could be listed as possible omissions from this study, the following may be noted: older writers of an earlier generation who continued to produce essays during the period under examination (Luis Alberto Sánchez of Peru and Arturo Uslar Pietri of Venezuela); younger essayists who began writing toward the end of our period (Mexico's Enrique Krauze and perhaps Hugo Hiriart); academics who have produced essays but whose literary activity has been carried on far from their native countries (Chile's Ariel Dorfman or Peru's Julio Ortega); and many journalists whose work at times approaches essayistic writing (Elena Poniatowska of Mexico or Argentina's Jacobo Timmerman would be good examples).

2. REVOLUTION OR REBELLION?

1. Paz, *Children of the Mire*, p. 154. Succeeding references appear parenthetically in the text as *CM*. Regarding my policy on the use of translations and translated titles, see "A Note on Translations" (following the acknowledgments).

2. Sábato, *Itinerario*, p. 154. This text appeared originally in 1963 in Sábato's *El escritor y sus fantasmas*.

3. A number of investigators have examined Paz's relationship to irrationalism and especially to the surrealists. Regarding this point, see Wilson, *Octavio Paz*, pp. 8–33, and Stabb, *In Quest of Identity*, pp. 198–200.

4. Cortázar, *Ultimo round*, p. 47. Succeeding references appear parenthetically in the text as *UR*. Note also that the original single-volume edition of this work (the edition I cite) was printed in a unique "two-story" format—independent split pages providing a larger "main floor" for some two-thirds of the material and a *planta baja*, or ground-floor, "bargain basement" for the remainder. My page references to the latter are prefaced by the letters "pb." Regarding possible thematic relationships between these two

"floors," see Stabb, "Not Text but Texture," p. 38, and Picón Garfield, *Cortázar por Cortázar*, p. 47.

5. Mafud, *Los argentinos y el status*, pp. 134–136, and Sebreli, *Mar del Plata*, p. 90. Succeeding references to the latter appear parenthetically in the text as *MP*.

6. An important exception might be David Viñas, who, in his novels of the period, seems especially sensitive to the mood of the younger generation.

7. Galeano, *Días y noches de amor y guerra*, p. 114. Succeeding references appear parenthetically in the text as *DN*.

8. Rangel, *Del buen revolucionario al buen salvaje*, p. 30. Succeeding references appear parenthetically in the text as *BR*.

9. See Reeve, "Carlos Fuentes como ensayista," pp. 2–3. Reeve holds that in the future Fuentes will come to be considered the most important essayist in Mexico after Reyes.

10. Villoro, "El sentido actual," unpaginated insert following p. 18.

11. Fuentes, "La máscara de esta década," p. vii.

12. García Ponce, *Desconsideraciones*, p. 66. Succeeding references appear parenthetically in the text as *DES*.

13. Monsiváis, "México 1967," p. iv.

14. Fuentes, "Carlos Fuentes habla de su vida," pp. vii-viii.

15. For a perceptive and very readable discussion of the Mexican political establishment, see Cosío Villegas's *El sistema político mexicano*.

16. Monsiváis, *Carlos Monsiváis*, p. 56.

17. Monsiváis, *Días de guardar*, p. 70. Succeeding references appear parenthetically in the text as *DG*.

18. Monsiváis, "México 1967," p. v.

19. Dallal, *Gozosa revolución*, p. 189.

20. Ibid., p. 223.

21. See especially Cosío Villegas's *Labor periodística*, pp. 140–142, 208–210, 320–322.

22. There is a rich bibliography dealing with Tlatelolco: for a helpful account of literary reactions to this event, see Young, "Mexican Literary Reactions," pp. 71–85.

23. In Young's study noted above there are virtually no texts mentioned—with the possible exception of Luis Spota's novel *La plaza* (1979)—that attempt to defend the position of the governmental authorities. See also Gyurko, "The Literacy Response to Nonoalco-Tlatelolco."

24. Fuentes's collagelike text "Paris: la revolución de Mayo" first appeared in *La Cultura en México*, July 31, 1968. Later that year Editorial Era reprinted it as a short book. While critics have compared it to Norman Mailer's *Armies of the Night*, I find its close resemblance to Julio Cortázar's "Noticias del mes de Mayo" quite remarkable. Cortázar's piece may be found in his collection *Ultimo round*.

25. Fuentes, *Tiempo mexicano*, p. 145. Succeeding references appear parenthetically in the text as *TM*.

26. Monsiváis, "México: notas," p. xvi.

27. Monsiváis, "La única cultura," p. iii.

28. Aguilar Mora, *La divina pareja*, p. 30.

29. Ibid., p. 69.

30. Monsiváis, *Amor perdido*, p. 252. Succeeding references appear parenthetically in the text as *AP*.

31. Mafud, *Socialismo del peronismo*, p. 9.

32. Mafud, *Psicología de la viveza criolla*, p. 65.

33. Mafud, *La revolución sexual argentina*, pp. 31–54.

34. Sebreli, *Eva Perón, ¿aventurera o militante?* pp. 27–28. Succeeding references appear parenthetically in the text as *EP*.

35. Sebreli, *Buenos Aires, vida cotidiana y alienación*, pp. 75ff. Succeeding references appear parenthetically in the text as *BA*.

36. Sebreli, *Mar del Plata: el ocio represivo*, p. 98. Succeeding references appear parenthetically in the text as *MP*.

37. The reference is to Juan Carlos Organía, military dictator of Argentina between 1966 and 1972.

38. Sebreli, *Fútbol y masas*, p. 153. Succeeding references appear parenthetically in the text as *FM*.

39. Sebreli refers specifically to an article by Sábato, who interpreted a victory of the Argentine "Racing" soccer team in international competition as giving the masses "faith in something." His reference to Galeano is in the form of a rejection of the latter's favorable comments on the game in his essay *Su majestad el fútbol*.

40. Mafud, *El hombre nuevo*, p. 81, passim.

41. For an interesting, though partisan, overview of liberation theology and its relationship to Latin American radicalism, see Berryman, *Liberation Theology*.

42. Cardenal, "Un marxismo con San Juan de la Cruz," pp. 40–45.

43. Sábato, *Itinerario*, p. 267.

44. There is a considerable bibliography on Victoria Ocampo. See especially Meyer, *Victoria Ocampo*, and Martin, *To Write Like a Woman*.

45. Castellanos, *El uso de la palabra*, p. 48. Succeeding references appear parenthetically in the text as *UP*.

46. Among the many comments on *El laberinto de la soledad*, see Wilson, *Octavio Paz*, pp. 50–51, and Stabb, *In Quest of Identity*, pp. 201–210.

47. Paz, *El laberinto de la soledad*, p. 182.

48. For further information on his sources for this essay, see Octavio Paz, *El ogro filantrópico*, p. 213, n. 2. Succeeding references to *El ogro filantrópico* appear parenthetically in the text as *OF*.

3. THE CULT OF PEPSICOÁTL

1. The late nineteenth and early twentieth centuries would appear to be the formative period for the development of these attitudes. The most influential and articulate Spanish American spokesman for "Latin culture" was José Enrique Rodó, whose essay *Ariel* became a vade mecum for a generation of intellectuals. Regarding this period, see Davis, *Latin American Thought*, pp. 174–181; Zum Felde, *Indice crítico*, pp. 289–330, and Stabb, *In Quest of Identity*, pp. 35–44.

2. Sebreli, *Tercer mundo, mito burgués*, p. 34. Succeeding references appear parenthetically in the text as *TMM*.

3. Sebreli, "No caer en la adoración de las masas," p. 32.

4. Ibid.

5. Rangel, *El tercermundismo*, pp. 61–65. Succeeding references appear parenthetically in the text as *T*.

6. Salazar Bondy, *Lima la horrible*, p. 49. Succeeding references appear parenthetically in the text as *LH*.

7. Sábato, *Apologías y rechazos*, p. 127. Succeeding references appear parenthetically in the text as *AR*.

8. Galeano, *Las venas abiertas de América Latina*, p. 256. Succeeding references appear parenthetically in the text as *VA*.

9. The nature of Mexican literary society has provided essayists, journalists, and other writers with relatively favorable conditions for the discussion and debate of these issues. By mid-century Mexico could boast a substantial reading public supporting numerous magazines and newspapers as well as a highly developed publishing industry. A popular essay in the Sunday supplement of *Excelsior* might have hundreds of thousands of readers; a text in the cultural section of a magazine such as *Siempre* might be perused by almost as many people; while more formal essays published in book form may, on occasion, warrant several printings of three to five thousand copies. Though these figures may not be comparable to similar statistics in the United States, they are impressive with respect to other Hispanic American countries. Other important—but less quantifiable—conditions contributing to the vitality of the Mexican essay (as well as other kinds of writing in the country) are national cohesiveness, political continuity, and the existence of relatively open dialogue regarding major issues.

10. Zaid, *El progreso improductivo*, p. 177. Succeeding references appear parenthetically in the text as *PI*.

11. Paz, *Posdata*, p. 74. Succeeding references appear parenthetically in the text as *P*.

4. THE TWILIGHT OF IDEOLOGY

1. Bell, *The End of Ideology*, p. 400. Succeeding references appear parenthetically in the text as *EI*.

2. For a contemporary Marxist definition of ideology in the context of Latin American letters, see Beverley and Zimmerman, *Literature and Politics in the Central American Revolutions*, pp. 1–7.

3. Mesa-Lago, *Revolutionary Change in Cuba*, p. 7.

4. To appreciate fully the mood of Mexican intellectuals at the birth of the new Cuba, see the effusive special number of the *Revista de la Universidad Nacional de México* titled "La revolución en Cuba" published in March 1959.

5. Donoso, *Historia personal del boom*, p. 57.

6. My reference here is to the ill-fated Spanish republic of the 1930s, nicknamed "the pretty girl" (*la niña bonita*) by politicians and writers of the period.

7. Guevara, *Obra revolucionaria*, p. 627. Succeeding references appear in the text as *OR*.

8. Benedetti, "Las prioridades del escritor en América Latina," p. 75.

9. Ibid., p. 71.

10. Ibid.

11. Fernández Retamar, *Ensayo de otro mundo*, p. 8.

12. Fernández Retamar, *Para el perfil definitivo del hombre*, p. 8.

13. Ibid., pp. 86–87.

14. Fernández Retamar, *Caliban and Other Essays*. Succeeding references appear parenthetically in the text as *C*.

15. Among the many items dealing with these events, see especially Menton, *Prose Fiction of the Cuban Revolution*, pp. 123–164; Casal, *El caso Padilla: literatura y revolución en Cuba*; and Mesa-Lago, *Revolutionary Change in Cuba*.

16. See also his *Para el perfil definitivo del hombre*, pp. 270–271, for a similar exposition of the same idea.

17. Earlier writers often expressed the same view: see especially Martínez Estrada's discussion of the Argentine rail system in his *Radiografía de la pampa*.

18. Galeano's devotion to the mystique of Marxism is also seen in his *Voces de nuestro tiempo*, pp. 27–48.

19. See especially his novel, *Libro de Manuel*, and his travel memoirs, *Nicaragua, tan violentamente dulce*.

20. Cortázar's text originally appeared in the Uruguayan periodical *Marcha*. Collazos then published it—along with his own article and a piece by Vargas Llosa—in a small book which bears the same title as Cortázar's contribution, *Literatura en la revolución y revolución en la literatura*. Succeeding references to the entire booklet appear parenthetically in the text as *LR*.

21. Cortázar's invented term *cronopio* is difficult to pin down precisely: it roughly stands for a "free spirit" and is usually a person of creative talent. For more on this term, see my discussion of his *Historias de cronopios y de famas* in chapter 5.

22. Upon the election of Argentina's democratic government in 1983, Sábato was chosen to head a national committee to investigate the *desaparecidos*—the "disappeared" victims of the previous military regimes.

23. My citation is from a later collection of previously published essays, *Itinerario*, p. 168.

24. Ibid., pp. 265–273.

25. Sábato, *Claves políticas*, p. 37.

26. Ibid., p. 50.

27. Sábato, *Apologías y rechazos*, p. 127.

28. Ibid., p. 166.

29. See chapter 3.

30. Sebreli, *El riesgo de pensar*, p. 132. Succeeding references appear parenthetically in the text as *RP*.

31. Edwards, *Persona non grata*, p. 6. Succeeding references appear parenthetically in the text as *PNG*.

32. Edwards, *Desde la cola del dragón*, p. 11. Succeeding references appear parenthetically in the text as *DC*.

33. Much of Vargas Llosa's essayistic work remains uncollected in such periodicals as the Peruvian *Oiga*, *Caretas*, the newspaper *El comercio*, as well as foreign journals of Paris, Mexico City, Caracas, Montevideo, and so on.

34. Vargas Llosa, *Entre Sartre y Camus*, p. 132. Succeeding references appear parenthetically in the text as *ESC*.

35. Vargas Llosa, *Contra viento y marea*, pp. 134–135.

36. At the risk of some misunderstanding, I am using the term "socialism" here as some Latin Americans and Europeans use it, that is, as synonymous with "communism" rather than denoting social democracy or groups similar to the American Socialist party.

37. Vargas Llosa's contribution is titled "Luzbel, Europa, y otras consideraciones." Its original date is April 1970 and it is included in the Collazos booklet *Literatura en la revolución*, pp. 78–93. See above, note 20. "Luzbel" is also reprinted in *Contra viento y marea*.

38. Regarding the Padilla affair, see above, note 15.

39. The texts and signatories of the two letters may be found in Casal, *El caso Padilla*, pp. 74, 123.

40. See chapter 2.

41. Vargas Llosa, *Contra viento y marea II*, pp. 260–278. Succeeding references appear parenthetically in the text as *CVM II*.

42. Beverley and Zimmerman, *Literature and Politics*, p. 21.

43. Vargas Llosa, "Como leer en bicicleta," pp. 76–78.

44. Zaid, *Como leer en bicicleta*, pp. 158–162. Succeeding references appear parenthetically in the text as *CLB*.

45. Zaid, "Carta polimétrica," pp. 46–47.

46. See chapter 2.

47. For a good discussion of Paz's relationship to surrealism, see Wilson, *Octavio Paz*, pp. 8–33.

48. For a discussion of these very early texts, see my *In Quest of Identity*, pp. 198–200.

49. Many contemporary feminists (and others) would, I think, find some confusion in Paz's apparent equation of *la rebelión erótica* and some very practical questions of sexual politics.

50. Paz, *Tiempo nublado*, p. 27. Succeeding references appear parenthetically in the text as *TN*.

5. TOWARD A NEW ESSAY

1. An interesting survey of experimental work in the essay may be seen in the anthology of American, British, and Continental writers by Kostelanetz, *Essaying Essays*. Kostelanetz's comments on formal innovations in the genre are germane to our study:

> Certain essayistic forms are not as new as they might initially seem. For instance, expository pastiche, which weaves quotations (and commentary) from disparate sources . . . rather closely resembles the traditional "commonplace" books, in which a discriminating, wisdom-loving author collected all the choice aphorisms and personal observations that he thought worth preserving . . .
> What is commonly called "the new journalism" represents an innovation not in essayistic form but in reportorial perspective, for its practitioners eschew pure objectivity to let their intelligences and emotional responses function actively . . . it is scarcely new in the tradition of essay-writing; even Montaigne, after all, was a rather active presence in his prose. (P. 5)

2. Adorno, *Teoría estética*, p. 267.

3. Only a few examples of the relationship between the two "floors" of *UR* can be cited: the boxing photos on pp. 13–14 of the *planta baja* and the upper-floor text bearing these page numbers; the *muñeca rota* text and illustrations on pp. 104–111 of both floors;

a tenuous thematic link between part of "La noche de Saint-Tropez" (pp. 137–143, *planta baja*) and "/que sepa abrir la puerta para ir a jugar" (pp. 141–154); and some intriguing parallels between the final pieces on both "floors"—Cortázar's impassioned self-defense in his open letter to Fernández Retamar (pp. 199–217, *planta baja*) and the brief but intriguingly titled "A los malos entendedores" (p. 217). Yet this evidence is not strong, especially in view of the fact that Cortázar himself maintains that the arrangement of the two "floors" was strictly "por azar" (by chance). Regarding this, see Picón Garfield, *Cortázar por Cortázar*, p. 47.

4. Cortázar, *La vuelta al día en ochenta mundos*. Succeeding references appear parenthetically in the text as *VDM*.

5. The English translation of this passage is from Peavler, *Julio Cortázar*, pp. 123–124.

6. An eloquent homage to Borges appears in Monterroso's *La palabra mágica*, p. 106.

7. One reference, however, is noteworthy. In his more recent confessional collage *La letra E* (1987), Monterroso recalls several meetings with Cortázar during the early eighties in Paris and Nicaragua. He also remembers visiting Cortázar's grave in the Montparnasse cemetery. On this occasion he makes a comment that cannot fail to strike a chord among those who know Cortázar's work well. He reveals that in the mid-1980s he just happened to be living in the apartment formerly occupied by the author of *Rayuela*: "here in this apartment (4 Rue Martel, 4th on the right) in which he lived and in which by chance coincidence worthy of his astute imagination I now live and am writing these lines."

8. It is of some significance that eight of the collection's ten titles begin with the letter O.

9. Cabrera Infante, *O*, p. 144. The Spanish word *politicastro* is a long-established term meaning a "cheap politician."

10. Ibid., p. 180.

11. Cabrera Infante, *Exorcismos de esti(l)o*, p. 18. Succeeding references appear parenthetically in the text as *EE*.

12. Regarding the term *cronopio*, see chapter 4, note 21.

13. The original publication of this text was in the journal *Buenos Aires Literaria*, pp. 32–37.

14. Cortázar, *Un tal Lucas*, pp. 43–45. Succeeding references appear in the text as *UTL*.

15. See, for example, his "La literatura de Tlatelolco." Note also the substratum of humor that defines his early novels as well as his later serious fiction. Regarding Ibargüengoitia's fiction, see Brushwood, *La novela mexicana: 1967–1982*.

16. Ibargüengoitia, *Viajes en la América ignota*, p. 143. Succeeding references appear parenthetically in the text as *V*.

17. For further discussion of the "porous text" notion, see Cortázar's essay "La muñeca rota" in *Ultimo round*.

18. More examples of the use of graffiti and slogans are noted in chapter 2.

19. The original Spanish line here is "La poesía es como un aire suave de pausados giros," an ironic echo of a familiar verse of Rubén Darío, Spanish America's most celebrated poet of the turn of the century.

20. An interesting discussion of what I have called the "*b*-game" appears in Brody, *Julio Cortázar: Rayuela*, pp. 60–61.

21. See my *Jorge Luis Borges*, pp. 94–100, and my *Borges Revisited*, p. 37.

22. Monterroso, *La palabra mágica*, pp. 106–111. The original date of this text is 1949.

23. The name of the publication, the magazine *Díalogos*, is mentioned in the text: "Futuro imposible" was, not surprisingly, originally published in *Díalogos* 36 (November–December 1970)!

24. Elizondo, *El grafógrafo*, p. 86.

25. The third category—the *esperanzas*—are only vaguely characterized. They may be somewhere between *famas* and *cronopios*, but the fact that Cortázar chose not to use them in his title perhaps indicates that they were stillborn in his conception of the text.

26. Cortázar, *Cronopios and Famas*, pp. 121–122.

27. Cortázar, *Vampiros multinacionales*, p. 41.

28. I refer here to Gregory Rabassa's fine translation, *A Certain Lucas*. Note, however, that I use my own translation of the original.

29. *El mono gramático* was first published in French in the prestigious Skira collection. As Jason Wilson points out, its original French title, *Le Singe grammairien*, lends itself to rich wordplay, as does the Spanish title (mono/grama). Regarding these possibilities, see Wilson, *Octavio Paz*, pp. 149–150. My references are to the English translation by Lane, *The Monkey Grammarian*: they appear parenthetically in the text as *MG*.

30. Wilson, *Octavio Paz*, p. 136.

31. Paz wrote *El mono gramático* while in residence at Harvard University in 1974–75.

32. Wilson, *Paz*, p. 151.

33. Cortázar's prefatory note regarding his sources merits inclusion here:

Las referencias al ciclo de las anguilas proceden de un artículo de Claude Lamotte publicado en *Le Monde*, Paris, 14 de abril de 1971; huelga decir que si alguna vez los ictiólogos allí citados leen estas páginas, cosa poco probable, no deberán ver en ellas la menor alusión personal: al igual que las anguilas, Jai Singh, las estrellas y yo mismo, son parte de una imagen que sólo apunta al lector.

34. Cortázar, *Prosa del observatorio*, p. 63. Succeeding references appear parenthetically in the text as *PO*.

35. Rossi, *Manual del distraído*, p. 7.

36. Elizondo, *El grafógrafo*, p. 9.

6. CONCLUSIONS

1. Regarding the relationship between postmodernism and contemporary Latin American letters, see Fokkema, *Literary History, Modernism and Postmodernism*, p. 38, and Hassan, "Pluralism in Modern Perspective," p. 18.

2. Regarding the question of identity during the mid-century, see my *In Quest of Identity*, pp. 146–220.

3. An excellent survey of this rich theme in Mexico may be found in Schmidt, *The Roots of Lo Mexicano*.

4. A few of the many periodicals in which the Mexican essayists have published include major journals of ideas such as *Plural* and *Vuelta*; smaller, more partisan reviews such as *Diálogos* or *Nexos*; the relatively staid *Revista de la Universidad de México*; and widely read popular publications such as *La Cultura en México*, the literary supplement of the magazine *Siempre*.

Bibliography

PRIMARY SOURCES: SPANISH AMERICAN ESSAYS

Aguilar Mora, Jorge. *La divina pareja: historia y mito*. Mexico City: Ediciones Era, 1978.

Benedetti, Mario. "Las prioridades del escritor en América Latina." *Casa de las Américas* 12, no. 68 (September–October 1971): 70–79.

Bryce Echenique, Alfredo. *A vuelo de buen cubero*. Barcelona: Angrama, 1977.

Cabrera Infante, Guillermo. *Exorcismos de esti(l)o*. Barcelona: Seix Barral, 1976.

———. *O*. Barcelona: Seix Barral, 1975.

Cardenal, Ernesto. "Un marxismo con San Juan de la Cruz." *Crisis* 14 (June 1974): 40–45.

Castellanos, Rosario. *El uso de la palabra*. 2d ed. Mexico City: Editores Mexicanos Unidos, 1987.

Collazos, Oscar, Julio Cortázar, and Mario Vargas Llosa. *Literatura en la revolución y revolución en la literatura: polémica*. Mexico City: Siglo Veintiuno, 1970.

Cortázar, Julio. *A Certain Lucas*. Translated by Gregory Rabassa. New York: Knopf, 1984.

———. *Cronopios and Famas*. Translated by Paul Blackburn. New York: Pantheon, 1969.

———. *Historias de cronopios y famas*. 2d ed. Buenos Aires: Minotauro, 1962.

———. *Prosa del observatorio*. Barcelona: Editorial Lumen, 1972.

———. *Un tal Lucas*. Madrid: Ediciones Alfaguara, 1984.

———. *Ultimo round*. Mexico City: Siglo Veintiuno, 1969.

———. *Vampiros multinacionales: una utopía realizable*. Mexico City: Excelsior, 1975.

———. *La vuelta al día en ochenta mundos*, 2 vols. Mexico City: Siglo Veintiuno, 1970.

Cosío Villegas, Daniel. *El estilo personal de gobernar*. Mexico City: J. Mortiz, 1974.

———. *El sistema político mexicano*. Mexico City: J. Mortiz, 1972.

———. *Labor periodística: real e imaginaria*. Mexico City: Era, 1972.

Dallal, Alberto. *Gozosa revolución*. Mexico City: UNAM, 1973.

Donoso, José. *The Boom in Spanish American Literature: A Personal History*. Translated by G. Kolovakos. New York: Columbia University Press, 1977.

———. *Historia personal del boom*. Barcelona: Anagrama, 1972.

Edwards, Jorge. *Desde la cola del dragón*. Barcelona: Dopesa, 1977.

———. *Persona non grata*. Barcelona: Barral Editores, 1973.

———. *Persona Non Grata*. Translated by Colin Harding. New York: Pomerica Press, 1976.

Elizondo, Salvador. *El grafógrafo*. Mexico City: J. Mortiz, 1978.

Fernández Retamar, Roberto. *Calibán: apuntes sobre la cultura de nuestra América*. Buenos Aires: La Pleyade, 1973.

———. *Caliban and Other Essays*. Translated by Edward Baker. Foreword by Frederic Jameson. Minneapolis: University of Minnesota Press, 1989.

———. *Ensayo de otro mundo*. Santiago de Chile: Editorial Universitaria, 1969.

———. *Para el perfil definitivo del hombre*. Havana: Letras Cubanas, 1981.

Fuentes, Carlos. "Carlos Fuentes habla de su vida . . . " *La Cultura en México*, September 29, 1965, pp. i–xii.

———. *Casa con dos puertas*. Mexico City: J. Mortiz, 1970.

———. "La máscara de esta década." *La Cultura en México*, July 3, 1963, pp. i–viii.

———. *La nueva novela hispanoamericana*. Mexico City: J. Mortiz, 1969.

———. *Tiempo mexicano*. Mexico City: J. Mortiz, 1971.

García Ponce, Juan. *Desconsideraciones*. Mexico City: J. Mortiz, 1968.

Galeano, Eduardo. *Días y noches de amor y guerra*. Havana: Casa de las Américas, 1978.

———. *Las venas abiertas de América Latina*. Mexico City: Siglo Veintiuno, 1971.

———. *Voces de nuestro tiempo*. San José: Editorial Universitaria Centroamericano, 1981.

Guevara, Ernesto. *Obra revolucionaria*. Prologue and selection by Roberto Fernández Retamar. Mexico City: Era, 1967.

Ibargüengoitia, Jorge. "La literatura de Tlatelolco." *Libro Abierto* 1 (1971): 38–40.

———. *Viajes en la América ignota*. Mexico City: J. Mortiz, 1972.

Kusch, Rodolfo. *De la mala vida porteña*. Buenos Aires: Peña Lillo, 1966.

Leñero, Vicente. *Los periodistas*. Mexico City: J. Mortiz, 1978.

Loayza, Luis. *El sol de Lima*. Lima: Mosca Azul, 1974.

Mafud, Julio. *Los argentinos y el status*. Buenos Aires: Americalee, 1966.

———. *El hombre nuevo: liberación y revolución*. Buenos Aires: Americalee, 1973.

———. *Psicología de la viveza criolla*. 5th ed. Buenos Aires: Americalee, 1973.

———. *La revolución sexual argentina*. Buenos Aires: Americalee, 1966.

———. *Sociología del peronismo*. Buenos Aires: Americalee, 1972.

Miró Quesada, Francisco. *Humanismo y revolución*. Lima: Casa de la Cultura del Perú, 1969.

Monsiváis, Carlos. *Amor perdido*. Mexico City: Era, 1978.

———. *Carlos Monsiváis*. In the series "Nuevos autores mexicanos presentados por sí mismos." Mexico City: Empresas Editoriales, 1966.

———. "Con un nuevo fracaso Carlos Monsiváis ayuda resquebrajar la máscara funeraria del mexicano." *La Cultura en México*, December 29, 1965, pp. ii–viii.

———. *Días de guardar*. Mexico City: Era, 1970.

————. "México 1967." *La Cultura en México*, January 17, 1968, pp. ii–vii.

————. "México: notas sobre literatura y sociedad." *La Cultura en México*, January 17, 1973, pp. ix–xvi.

————. "La única cultura capaz de sacarnos del subdesarollo ha perdido una batalla." *La Cultura en México*, April 17, 1966, pp. iii–iv.

Monterroso, Augusto. *La letra E.* Mexico City: Era, 1987.

————. *La palabra mágica.* Mexico City: Era, 1983.

————. *Lo demás es silencio.* Barcelona: Seix Barral, 1978.

Paz, Octavio. *Children of the Mire: Modern Poetry from Romanticism to the Avant-Garde.* Translated by Rachel Phillips. Cambridge: Harvard University Press, 1974.

————. *Los hijos del limo.* Barcelona: Seix Barral, 1974.

————. *El laberinto de la soledad.* 2d ed., revised and enlarged. Mexico City: Fondo de Cultura Económica, 1959.

————. *The Monkey Grammarian.* Translated by Helen R. Lane. New York: Seaver Books, 1981.

————. *El mono gramático.* Barcelona: Seix Barral, 1974.

————. *El ogro filantrópico.* Barcelona: Seix Barral, 1979.

————. *Posdata.* Mexico City: Siglo Veintiuno, 1970.

————. *Tiempo nublado.* Barcelona: Seix Barral, 1983.

Poniatowska, Elena. *La noche de Tlatelolco: testimonios de historia oral.* Mexico City: Era, 1972.

Rangel, Carlos. *Del buen salvaje al buen revolucionario.* Caracas: Monte Avila, 1976.

————. *El tercermundismo.* Caracas: Monte Avila, 1982.

Ribeyro, Julio Ramón. *Prosas apátridas.* Barcelona: Tusquets, 1975.

Romero, José. *Latinoamerica: las ciudades y las ideas.* Buenos Aires: Siglo Veintiuno, 1976.

Rossi, Alejandro. *Manual del distraído.* Mexico City: J. Mortiz, 1978.

Sábato, Ernesto. *Apologías y rechazos.* Barcelona: Seix Barral, 1979.

————. *Claves políticas.* Buenos Aires: El Escarabajo de Oro, 1971.

————. *Itinerario.* Buenos Aires: Sur, 1969.

Salazar Bondy, Sebastián. *Lima la horrible.* 3d ed. Mexico City: Era, 1968.

Sarduy, Severo. *Barroco.* Buenos Aires: Sudamericana, 1974.

Sebreli, Juan José. *Buenos Aires, vida cotidiana y alienación.* Buenos Aires: Siglo XX, 1965.

————. *Los deseos imaginarios del peronismo.* Buenos Aires: Legaza, 1983.

————. *Eva Perón, ¿aventurera o militante?* Buenos Aires: Siglo XX, 1966.

————. *Fútbol y masas.* Buenos Aires: Galerna, 1981.

————. *Mar del Plata: el ocio represivo.* Buenos Aires: Tiempo Contemporáneo, 1970.

————. "No caer en la adoración de las masas." *Crisis* 41 (April 1986): 32–33.

————. *El riesgo de pensar: ensayos 1950–1984.* Buenos Aires: Sudamericana, 1984.

————. *Tercer mundo, mito burgués.* Buenos Aires: Siglo XX, 1965.

Vargas Llosa, Mario. *Contra viento y marea.* Barcelona: Seix Barral, 1983.

————. *Contra viento y marea II: 1972–1983.* Barcelona: Seix Barral, 1986.

————. *Entre Sartre y Camus.* San Juan: Huracán, 1981.

Villoro, Luis. "El sentido actual de la filosofía en México." *Revista de la Universidad de México* 22 (January 1968): unpaginated insert following p. 18.

Zaid, Gabriel. "Carta polimétrica." *Vuelta* 4 (March 1980): 46–47.

————. *Como leer en bicicleta: problemas de la cultura en México.* 2d ed. corrected and enlarged. Mexico City: J. Mortiz, 1979.

————. *El progreso improductivo.* Mexico City: Siglo Veintiuno, 1979.

SECONDARY SOURCES

Adorno, Theodor. *Teoría estética.* Castilian version by F. Riaza. Madrid: Taurus, 1971.

Bell, Daniel. *The End of Ideology: On the Exhaustion of Political Ideas in the Fifties.* Glencoe, Ill.: Free Press, 1960.

Berryman, Phillip. *Liberation Theology.* New York: Pantheon, 1987.

Beverley, John, and Marc Zimmerman. *Literature and Politics in Central American Revolutions.* Austin: University of Texas Press, 1990.

Brody, Robert. *Julio Cortázar: Rayuela.* London: Grant and Cutler, 1976.

Brushwood, John S. *La novela mexicana: 1967–1982.* Mexico City: Grijalbo, 1985.

Casal, Lourdes. *El caso Padilla: literatura y revolución en Cuba.* Miami: Universal, 1971.

Chadbourne, Richard M. "A Puzzling Literary Genre: Comparative Views of the Essay." *Comparative Literature Studies* 20, no. 2 (Summer 1983): 133–153.

Davis, Harold E. *Latin American Thought: A Historical Introduction.* Baton Rouge: Louisiana State University Press, 1972.

Earle, Peter G. "On the Contemporary Displacement of the Hispanic American Essay." *Hispanic Review* 46 (1978): 329–341.

Fokkema, Douwe W. *Literary History, Modernism and Post-modernism.* Amsterdam and Philadelphia: J. Benjamins, 1984.

Gómez Martínez, José L. "Teoría y ensayo: un estudio bibliográfico." *Cuadernos Salmantinos de Filosofía* 4 (1978): 313–328.

Gyurko, Lanin A. "The Literary Response to Nonoalco-Tlatelolco." In *Contemporary Latin American Culture.* Edited by C. G. Gunterman, pp. 45–77. Tempe: Arizona State University Press, 1984.

Hassan, Ihab. "Pluralism in Modern Perspective." In *Exploring Postmodernism.* Edited by Douwe W. Fokkema. Amsterdam and Philadelphia: J. Benjamins, 1987.

Kostelanetz, Richard. *Essaying Essays: Alternate Forms of Exposition.* New York: Out of London Press, 1975.

Loveluck, Juan. "Esquividad y concreción del ensayo." *Literatura Chilena* 23 (October–December 1982): 2–7.

Martin, Leona. "To Write Like a Woman: Gender Inflection in the Prose of Victoria Ocampo." Ph.D. dissertation. Ann Arbor: University Microfilms 91–04923, 1991.

Martínez, José Luis. *El ensayo mexicano moderno.* 2d ed. Mexico City: Fondo de Cultura Económica, 1971.

Menton, Seymour. *Prose Fiction of the Cuban Revolution.* Austin: University of Texas Press, 1975.

Mesa-Lago, Carmelo, ed. *Revolutionary Change in Cuba.* Pittsburgh: University of Pittsburgh Press, 1971.

Meyer, Doris. *Victoria Ocampo: Against the Wind and Tide.* New York: George Braziller, 1979.

Peavler, Terry. *Julio Cortázar.* Boston: Twayne, 1990.

Picón Garfield, Evelyn. *Cortázar por Cortázar.* Xalapa: Universidad Veracruzana, 1981.

Reeve, Richard. "Carlos Fuentes como ensayista." *Revista de la Universidad de México* 24, (January–February 1970): 2–3.

Roy, Joaquín. "Periodismo y ensayo." In *El ensayo hispánico*. Acts of a symposium on the Hispanic essay. Edited by Isaac J. Levy and Juan Loveluck. Columbia: University of South Carolina Press, 1984.

Sacoto, Antonio. "El ensayo hispanoamericano contemporáneo." *Cuadernos Americanos (Nueva Epoca)* 3, no. 9 (May–June 1988): 107–120.

Scholes, Robert, and Karl Klaus. *Elements of the Essay*. New York: Oxford, 1968.

Schmidt, Henry C. *The Roots of Lo Mexicano: Self and Society in Mexican Thought, 1900–1934*. College Station and London: Texas A & M Press, 1978.

Skirius, John. *El ensayo hispanoamericano del siglo XX*. Mexico City: Fondo de Cultura Económica, 1981.

Stabb, Martin S. *Borges Revisited*. Boston: Twayne, 1991.

―――. *In Quest of Identity: Patterns in the Spanish American Essay of Ideas, 1890–1960*. Chapel Hill: University of North Carolina Press, 1967.

―――. *Jorge Luis Borges*. New York: Twayne, 1970.

―――. "The New Essay of Mexico: Text and Context." *Hispania* 70 (March 1987): 47–60.

―――. "Not Text but Texture: Cortázar and the New Essay." *Hispanic Review* 52 (Spring 1984): 19–40.

Victoria, Marcos. *Teoría del ensayo*. Buenos Aires: Emecé, 1974.

Wilson, Jason. *Octavio Paz: A Study of His Poetics*. Cambridge, London, New York, and Melbourne: Cambridge University Press, 1979.

Young, Dolly J. "Mexican Literary Responses to Tlatelolco, 1968." *Latin American Research Review* 20 (1965): 71–85.

Zum Felde, Alberto. *Indice crítico de la literatura hispano-americana: el ensayo y la crítica*. Mexico City: Guarania, 1954.

Index